Biblical Sermons

Biblical

How Twelve Preachers Apply the Principles of *Biblical Preaching*

Sermons

Haddon W. Robinson

BAKER BOOK HOUSE
Grand Rapids, Michigan 49516

©1989 by Baker Book House Company

Published by Baker Books
a division of Baker Book House Company
P.O. Box 6287, Grand Rapids, MI 49516-6287

First cloth edition published in 1989 by Baker Book House Company

First paperback edition published in 1997 by Baker Book House Company

Third printing, March 2000

Printed in the United States of America

Library of Congress Cataloging-in-Publication Data

Biblical sermons.

    Consists of twelve sermons by various preachers; commentary on the sermons and interviews with the preachers by Haddon W. Robinson.
    Includes index.
    1. Sermons, American. 2. Sermons—History and criticism. I. Robinson, Haddon W.
BV4241.B46   1989   252   89-248
ISBN 0-8010-9044-X

For information about academic books, resources for Christian leaders, and all new releases available from Baker Book House, visit our web site:
http://www.bakerbooks.com

Contents

Introduction   7

	Sermon	Commentary	Interview
1. A Case Study in Temptation, *Genesis 3:1–6* *Haddon W. Robinson*	13	23	27
2. Thou Shalt Not Commit Adultery, *Exodus 20:14* *Erwin W. Lutzer*	31	41	45
3. The Big Valley, *1 Samuel 17:1–51* *James O. Rose*	51	61	65
4. A Night in Persia, *Esther* *Donald Sunukjian*	69	81	85
5. Riding the Wind of God, *Psalm 127* *Duane Litfin*	89	105	109
6. He Who Has Ears to Hear . . . , *Jeremiah 1* *Bo Matthews*	113	123	127
7. For "Wait" Watchers Only! *Luke 1:5–25* *George Kenworthy*	133	143	147
8. Who Cares? *Luke 15* *Joseph M. Stowell*	151	167	173
9. A Woman Who Came a Stone's Throw from Death, *John 8:1–12* *Nancy Hardin*	179	193	197
10. How to Stand Perfect in the Sight of God, *Romans 4:5* *Larry Moyer*	201	213	217

Contents

11. When Life Deals You a Lemon,
    Make a Lemonade, *James*   221   231   235
    Michael Cocoris

12. Lament for the City of Man,
    Revelation 17–18   239   255   259
    Joel Eidsness

    List of Sermon Illustrations   263
    Index   264

Introduction

Several years ago I took a course in geology. More accurately, the course took me. Our class met for three lectures each week plus a lab session. The professor lectured about rocks and rock formations, and in the assigned reading we were provided with descriptions of rocks and photographs of what they looked like. On the examinations based on the lectures and the textbook, I received high grades—which demonstrates only that professional students learn how to listen and read.

It was the lab sessions that did me in! There we faced real rocks. We were required to identify the igneous, sedimentary, and metamorphic rocks and to pick out the silicates, carbonates, and sulphides as well. I labeled four out of ten correctly, a percentage slightly worse than could be achieved by flipping a coin. Obviously, I had rocks in my head, but that did not transfer to the rocks I held in my hand!

With that geology class still an uncomfortable memory, I empathized with the reactions of a few of the homiletics professors using my book *Biblical Preaching* as a text.[1] "Students need to see the principles in practice," they wrote. "If there's anyone out there who practices what you teach, have them provide some sermons as examples."

As a result of such prodding, I contacted several former stu-

1. Haddon W. Robinson, *Biblical Preaching: The Development and Delivery of Expository Messages* (Grand Rapids: Baker, 1980).

dents who, for better or worse, carry the smudge of my thumb-print upon them, and I asked for a specimen sermon. None of these preachers jumped at the opportunity. A couple of them protested that any sermons they provided would only end up as bad examples. Their modesty is both commendable and under-standable. While all of these ministers have been preaching for over a decade and have reputations as effective communicators, they don't consider themselves pulpit masters. Therefore, some-thing needs to be said in their defense.

First, this book is not an anthology of "The Greatest Sermons of the Twentieth Century." In fact, these sermons do not neces-sarily represent the best work of these preachers. All of these messages were forged out of the demanding routines of busy ministries. Most of the contributors serve as active pastors. One travels as an evangelist. I put in time as a seminary president. One, a woman, is regularly involved in women's conferences. All would vote for a twenty-eight-hour day and an eight-day week. While the sermons may have received a bit more polish than usual, each smacks of the ordinary rather than the extraordinary and represents what preaching done on a regular basis looks like. Yet, the sermons also demonstrate that ministers living with the pressures of demanding schedules and the tensions of mod-ern society can still preach helpful biblical messages when they meet their congregations on Sunday.

Second, sermons are designed to be heard—not read. A ser-mon on the page is like a figure in a wax museum. The form stands there, but the flash of the eye, the language of the face, the sweep of the hand, the range of the voice, the life and breath are missing. Sermons are never preached in cold blood. All of these ministers sound better than their printed sermons. What is more, the stronger the preacher, the greater the contrast be-tween his manuscript and his spoken word. Yet, printed sermons do have value. Admittedly, a biology student takes the life of the frog when she dissects it in the laboratory, but she studies the parts, nonetheless, to discover what makes a frog jump. A student of preaching can discover in the sermon on a page what might never emerge listening to the same sermon from the pulpit.

While dissecting a written sermon omits the important ingredient of the word spoken, it remains an effective way to analyze how sermons are put together.

Third, while all of the contributors have been my students, some practice the methodology that I have taught more extensively than others. All endorse my approach and recommend it, but as John Nicholls Booth noted in the introduction to his little book, *The Quest for Preaching Power*: "Rules for preaching are simply the scaffolding used during the construction period. In the building years of one's ministry, sermons must be erected within this protecting, guiding structure. Later the form to follow becomes ingrained and the scaffolding may be torn down, completely forgotten."[2] None of these preachers is a clone of mine. While they have accepted my philosophy of homiletics, they have benefited from the counsel of others and from experience. Shaped by their reading and their own background and pilgrimage, their preaching reaches beyond any static rules to reflect their own personalities. While no good preacher outgrows the principles and devices of the preaching art, as a skilled, experienced craftsman, each has developed beyond them.

The purpose of this book, therefore, is to demonstrate how the approach to homiletics in *Biblical Preaching* is worked out in sermons of several experienced communicators. Since much of homiletics is more caught than taught, these ministers show us a specimen of the work they have done and thus let us glimpse how they work.

Many different pressures work on a minister as he or she crafts a sermon. First, the biblical material exerts its force. The sermons in this book expound texts from Genesis to Revelation. The collection embraces an impressive variety of biblical genre—narrative, poetry, history, law, parables, letters, and apocalyptic literature. The Bible not only supplies the central idea and supporting content for each lesson, but usually dictates its form as well. Had these preachers based their sermons on another bib-

---

2. John Nicholls Boothe, *The Quest for Preaching Power* (New York: Macmillan, 1943), p. xv.

lical passage, each might have approached the text in a completely different manner.

A second factor present in the development of a sermon is the audience. Sermons, unlike essays, are not addressed "to whom it may concern"; they are delivered to men and women sitting at a certain time of day, usually on Sunday in a building with a zip code. Since these congregations exist in the latter half of the twentieth century, they possess much in common. Although situated in different parts of the United States and carrying a variety of denominational labels, they represent predominantly upper-working-class and middle-class churches. All are strongly evangelical. Yet, each congregation, while affected by the winds which sweep across American society, is also unique in its own temptations, pain, and frustrations. When the pastor stands to preach, it is to that particular people he must speak. The congregation has been with him in the study during the preparation of the message. Each preacher has invested time in the passage, often reading it in the original languages. He has brought down from the shelf the reference books and consulted the commentaries. While each minister teaches his congregation the Bible, he does not serve as their professor but as their pastor. His sanctuary is not a seminary, and his audience will not be expected to pass an examination on the content. As Ruskin said, he has "thirty minutes to raise the dead"[3] and to persuade his hearers to let the Bible into their lives. Each minister wants to be faithful to the text and to scholarly discussions about the passage, but, above all, he desires to be faithful to his people. Sermons, therefore, are more like thoughtful conversations than scholarly lectures.

Any preacher who prepares forty to a hundred sermons a year knows the weasel sameness that sucks life from a message. Sermons hammered together like a doghouse each week are a burden to preach and a chore for a congregation to hear. Unfortunately, "the great awakening" in some churches is not a period of history but the moment when the sermon ends and

---

3. Quoted in Donald Miller, *Fire in Thy Mouth* (Nashville: Abingdon, 1954), p. 17.

the congregation stands for the final hymn. Perceptive preachers know that variety is not only the spice of life, but of preaching as well. Some of the sermons in this book are deductive, some inductive, and at least one semi-inductive. Two expound a single verse, others work through a paragraph or series of paragraphs, and two cover an entire book of the Bible. In their unfolding they explain ideas, prove propositions, and apply principles. Three narrate stories, but from different perspectives. One tells an incident through the eyes of a biblical character, while another looks at history from the perspective of an imaginary participant.

Variety extends to the details of the sermon. You will find it in the word pictures, illustrations drawn from the range of life, statements from authorities, dialogue, and humor. Yet all the preachers strive to be biblical and faithful to the text. The sermons demonstrate that preaching takes many forms and does not have to be "the art of talking in someone else's sleep."

A reading of these sermons can benefit us personally. Since the reader and the original hearers share a common humanity, what was originally intended for one audience can enrich another. These sermons, therefore, should be read listening for a word from God.

Studying the sermons can expose a student to the different forms sermons take. Sermons have no standard form. Only their content and purpose make them what they are. While Christian preaching has developed under the strong influence of Greek and Roman rhetoric, no biblical mandate demands that sermons take that prescribed form. In fact, the teachers and prophets in the Scriptures used parables, narratives, poems, riddles, speeches, letters, and visual aids to communicate their ideas. They simply asked, "What do I say to this audience through what channel for what purpose, for what effect?" and they said it.

These sermons can also illustrate many of the principles discussed in *Biblical Preaching*. In my evaluation of each sermon, I attempt to underline the strengths of that particular sermon, but a perceptive student will discover other things the preacher did well and, since the sermons come from the quarry without much polish, will find some rough parts that need more work. Few of us preach textbook sermons every Sunday.

The interview with each contributor tries to probe what ministers do and how they think as they prepare to speak. The conversations took place over the telephone and then were edited; nonetheless, they provide a bit of insight to the preacher's method of preparation and what it takes to put a sermon together. Each preacher comes at the task in a different way, and seeing that may set a reader free to find ways of working that fit his or her personality.

Many people have put themselves on the line and put themselves out to put this book together. I am honored beyond words by these former students, now friends, who have submitted sermons to the collection. Seminary teaching does not have many immediate rewards, but one payoff comes in seeing students develop beyond their professors.

George Kenworthy deserves special thanks for his valuable assistance. He prodded me into putting the book together, worked with the contributors, submitted a sermon, and offered his help at every turn. His name should be on the cover. It is written on my heart.

Lori Seath typed and retyped the manuscript and did it with patience and pretended joy. Only those who have written a book themselves know what service like that means. Alice Mathews read the manuscript and gave her candid reaction. I decided to publish the book anyhow.

The sermons could have been arranged in several different ways. I've chosen to present them the way the texts appear in the Bible, starting with Genesis and ending with Revelation. At the end of the book I've included a subject index that will guide the reader to particular types of sermons and comments on particular parts of sermons such as introductions and conclusions.

Chapter 1

A Case Study in Temptation
Genesis 3:1–6

Haddon W. Robinson

A few months ago I received a letter from a young man in a penitentiary in Texas. He is serving from ten to twenty years for attempted rape. He is a Christian, and he asked if I would send him a book that was not available to him in the prison. I gladly responded to his request. But his letter deeply disturbed me, because the young man had been a student of mine when he was in seminary.

When he left the seminary, he left with notable gift and great vision. He pastored two different churches, and both of them, humanly speaking, were successful congregations. In the second church, which I knew better, he demonstrated the gift of evangelism. Many of the people in that church were led to Christ as a result of his witness. He was a careful student of the Scriptures. There were those in the congregation who testified that again and again as he stood to speak they could sense the power and the presence of God. He had a discipling ministry; he left his thumbprint upon the men in that congregation. In fact, when his crime was discovered and he had admitted his guilt, men in his church raised over $20,000 for his legal defense. And now he is a prisoner in a penitentiary in Texas. In one dark hour of temptation he fell into the abyss. He ruined his reputation, destroyed his ministry, and left an ugly stain on the testimony of Christ in that community.

When I read that letter and knew what had happened, I found myself wrestling with all kinds of questions and emotions. What happens in a person's life who does that? What went through his mind? What was it that caused him to turn his back on all that he had given his life to?

I realized as I was asking those questions that I was not simply asking about him, but about myself. I was asking about men and women who have graduated from seminary who, in some act of disobedience, have destroyed the ministry to which they have given themselves. What is it that causes someone to mortgage his ministry to pay the high price of sin? What is it that lures us to destruction?

It's a question you face. You're a Christian. Temptation dogs your path and trips you at every turn. The question you must face sometime in your life is, "How does the tempter do his work? How does he come to us? How does he destroy us?" Here, early in the ancient record, we have one of the themes that appears again and again throughout the Scripture, the theme of sin and its destructive power.

What we have here in Genesis 3 is a case study in temptation. In a case study, you get rid of the independent variables to study the thing itself. As Eve is approached by the tempter, many things are true of her that are not true of us. For example, she has no poisoned blood in her veins. She does not have a heritage on which she can blame her sin. Eve comes, as Adam does, as the direct creation of God; and when God created Adam and Eve, God declared that the creation was very good. Unlike people today, Adam and Eve were not half-damned at birth. What is more, Eve and Adam lived in a perfect environment. Nothing in the pollution of that atmosphere would lead them away from God. So Eve stands in the morning of creation, a creature of great wonder. No sinful heritage, no savaged environment. We have a case study in temptation.

As we watch the way the tempter comes to Eve, we recognize

that while this story comes to us out of the ancient past, it's as up-to-date as the temptation you faced last night—the temptation you may be feeling this morning, the temptation you face in your study, in your home, in your ministry, in your life. The scene has changed, but the methodology has not.

As you read this story, one thing is obvious. When the tempter comes, he comes to us in disguise. The writer of Genesis notes the serpent was "more crafty than any of the wild animals the Lord God had made." When the serpent approached, therefore, he did not come as a creature of ugliness. This scene happens before the curse, before the serpent crawls on its belly over the ground. No rattlers here warn of an approaching danger. There's nothing here that would make Eve feel alarmed.

When Satan comes to you, he does not come in the form of a coiled snake. He does not approach with the roar of a lion. He does not come with the wail of a siren. He does not come waving a red flag. Satan simply slides into your life. When he appears, he seems almost like a comfortable companion. There's nothing about him that you would dread. The New Testament warns that he dresses as an angel of light, a servant of God, a minister of righteousness. One point seems quite clear: when the enemy attacks you, he wears a disguise. As Mephistopheles says in *Faust,* "The people do not know the devil is there even when he has them by the throat."

Not only is he disguised in his person, but he disguises his purposes. He does not whisper to Eve, "I am here to tempt you." He merely wants to conduct a religious discussion. He would like to discuss theology; he doesn't intend to talk about sin. The serpent opens the conversation by asking, "Did God really say, 'You must not eat from any tree in the garden'?" You can't argue with that. Satan asks only for clarification. "Look, I want to be sure of your exegesis. I want to understand the idea God was trying to get across. Did he really say you can't eat of any of the trees of the garden?" You see, he is a religious devil. He doesn't come and knock on the door of your soul and say, "Pardon me, buddy, allow me a half hour of your life. I'd like to damn and destroy you." No, all he wants to do is talk about a point of theology. He only desires to interpret the Word of God. It is possible, isn't it, to discuss theology to our peril. We can talk about God in an abstract way, as though he were a mathematical formula. You can concoct a theology that leads you to disobey God.

You're convinced about grace, very strong on Christian liberty. You know the freedom of the sons and daughters of God and you will debate grace with anyone. You can do anything you want, at any time you want, with anyone you want. No restrictions, no hangups; you're free; you know God's grace! Every person who's ever turned liberty into license has done so on theological grounds. "Even when I sin, God's grace abounds. Isn't it wonderful that I always have God's grace because when I sin, I demonstrate his forgiveness?"

You can be strong on God's sovereignty. No one will outpace you when it comes to that doctrine. God is sovereign over the affairs of men and nations. God's eye is not only over history; his hand is on history. His hand rests upon your life, but before long God is so sovereign that you have no responsibility. In a sense "all the world's a stage, all the men and women merely players." God maps out the action, plans the dialogue. We go through our paces, but it's all of God. Even our sin. And out of that discussion you find good sound reasons—or reasons that sound good—for disobeying God. All because you discuss theology with the wrong motive. One advantage of graduating from seminary is that you can manufacture a lot of pious excuses for doing wrong and be theological in your disobedience.

Another thing that Satan does in this conversation, this discussion about God, is to focus Eve's attention on that single tree in the center of the garden. He says, "It is inconceivable to me that God wouldn't let you have any of these trees." Now Eve jumps to God's defense. She's a witness on behalf of God. "No, we can eat of all of the trees in the garden but that one tree—that tree there in the center—we can't eat from that, we can't touch that tree." God didn't say that. He didn't say anything about "touching" it. Some people defend God by becoming stricter than God. They not only know God's commands, but they believe they are holier if they go beyond those commands. There is danger in that. Eve says, "You know we can't taste it; we can't even touch it." What Satan has done, of course, is to focus her mind on that single tree, the one thing God prohibited.

Sometimes people turn their backs on all the good things, all the blessings that have been poured into their lives—throw all that away for a single sin in their lives. They no longer can see God's goodness. Satan shifts your focus, and there emerges that one thing you want so desperately, you'll do anything to get it. It becomes the obsession of your life, and everything else God does for you, you forget. So Satan comes in disguise. He conceals who he is. He conceals what he wants to do.

The second part of his strategy is to attack God's Word. When Eve responds, "We may eat from all the trees in the garden, but we must not eat the fruit from the tree that's in the middle of the garden. We must not touch it or we will die," then Satan throws his head back and with irrepressible laughter says, "Surely you don't believe that, do you? That you will surely die? Oh, come now. A bit of fruit? Surely die? That's just a bit of exaggeration God's using to get your attention. He doesn't mean that. Surely die? You're too sophisticated to believe that God who gave you this marvelous garden and all these trees, and that bountiful fruit is going to be that upset about your taking that one piece of fruit. Surely die? You can't be serious! God doesn't mean that. God certainly doesn't mean that."

I can believe in the inerrancy of the Bible as a whole, except on one particular issue between God and me; I'm sure God doesn't mean it when he says, "You will surely die."

For thousands of years Satan has repeated that strategy. It is the theme of modern novels. The author manipulates the plot so that his characters live in deep disobedience against God, yet at the end everything has turned out well. It's the subject of modern movies in which the characters rebel against the moral laws of God but live happily ever after. It's the word from the sponsor on television. It appears in four-color ads. Here's a perfume—it's been on the market for a long time—called "My Sin." A huckster on Madison Avenue named that fragrance. "Here is a fragrance that is so alluring, so charming, so exciting," he whispers, "we can call it 'My Sin.'" You would never guess the fragrance of sin arises as a stench in the nostrils of God.

How do you respond to the warnings against disobedience that fill the pages of Scripture? Does God mean it when he says, "The mind of sinful man is death"? Does God mean it when he declares, "The one who sows to please his sinful nature, from that nature will reap destruction"? Does God mean it when he urges, "Do not be deceived: God cannot be mocked. A man reaps what he sows"? Does God mean it when he states, "But all the wicked he will destroy"? Does God mean it when he warns, "The LORD will judge his people"? Does God mean it when he promises, "God will judge the adulterer and all the sexually immoral"? Does God mean it when he tells us that sin brings punishment?

God is serious about sin because God is serious about you. God is serious about sin because he loves you and knows the devastation that sin can bring in your life, in your relationships, in your character, in your ministry. God is serious about sin as a loving parent is serious about fire and warns a child about it, knowing that it can maim that child for life, destroy the home he lives in, and do untold damage. But how do you feel about it? Do you take God seriously when he utters those warnings?

Not only does Satan attack God's Word, but he drives deeper and attacks God's character, which lies behind his Word. The serpent explains to the woman, "For God knows that when you eat of it [that tree] your eyes will be opened, and you will be like God, knowing good and evil." Satan slanders God's goodness. He implies, "Do you know why God gave you that command? He wants to spoil your fun. He wants to hold you on a tight leash. He doesn't want you to be free and experience the good life. He is out to deny you pleasures. He desires to keep you down. He wants to forbid you the excitement that life offers. He knows very well that when you eat that fruit, you'll be like him and will know good and evil. Then you'll enjoy experiences beyond your wildest dreams. God has an ulterior motive, a hidden agenda, and it's an evil one."

Once the well is poisoned, all the water is polluted. One of the most beautiful confessions of love and faith in the Bible is the confession Ruth makes to Naomi. June embraces November. Ruth pleads, "Don't urge me to leave you or to turn back from you. Where you go I will go, and where you stay I will stay. Your people will be my people and your God my God. Where you die I will die, and there I will be buried." An expression of loyal devotion as beautiful as any in all of literature.

But suppose someone whispered to Naomi, "Naomi, listen. Ruth's a gold digger. She's a manipulator. What Ruth, this Moabitess, really wants is to get into Israel and marry a wealthy Jew. She knows you are her passport. She'll tell you anything to get a visa into Israel." If Naomi believed that, the well is poisoned. Every good word Ruth speaks, Naomi now suspects. Every kind act Ruth does, Naomi will reject. When you poison the well, all the water is contaminated. If you question God's Word because you doubt God's goodness, then Satan has done his work. How easily we succumb. All of us have served the Prince of Darkness and lived in his realm too long. When we enter the kingdom of God's Son, we carry our doubts and suspicions with us. If something painful happens in our lives, we ask "why?" and the question mark is like a dagger pointed at the heart of God. How easily we suspect that when some reversal happens in our lives, God has lined up against us. We suffer such a twisted will that even when good things happen to us we doubt God's goodness. If something marvelous comes into our life, something completely unexpected, at first we're delighted. Then all at once a shadow crosses our mind that it will soon be snatched away. God doesn't really want me to enjoy this expression of his goodness; just as I start to enjoy it, he'll pull it back like a sadistic parent. So we "knock on wood" and hammer at the heart of God. When we doubt God's goodness, we will doubt his Word. If we believe God wants to hold us back from enjoying a full life, then the work of the tempter is complete.

At that moment, "when the woman saw that the fruit of the tree was good for food and pleasing to the eye, and also desirable for gaining wisdom, she took some and ate it." Now the forbidden fruit pleases her eye. She has listened to the lie of the tempter and her senses take control. When you get God out of your life, if you come to question God's Word and God's goodness, then your senses come alive to what is evil; what was once out of bounds to you becomes what you desire more than anything else on earth, even if it is something that can destroy you.

"Piece of fruit?" someone might say. "Surely not a piece of fruit. You're not going to tell me that Eve sinned by eating a piece of fruit in the orchard. You're not going to tell me that's why Adam sinned and why murder came into their family. You're not going to tell me a piece of fruit damned the race."

No, not a piece of fruit, but disobedience to God's Word, an ugly suspicion of God's character. The fruit is out at the periphery; the sin stands at the center. Whenever you come to doubt or deny the goodness of God, then at that point you'll come to reject his Word—the fruit is only the point of disobedience.

SERMON

22

If Satan had come to Eve that early morning and said, "Look, sign this paper. Say that you are through with God," she would never have signed it. When Satan approaches us, he never comes dragging the chains that will enslave us. He comes bringing a crown that will ennoble us. He comes offering us pleasure, expansiveness, money, popularity, freedom, and joy. In fact, he never hints about the consequences; he only promises we will fill all the desires of our hearts. That is how we are destroyed. That's the lesson: the temptations that destroy us strike at the heart of God, at God's integrity and God's goodness. As we deny God's goodness, we reject his Word. When we reject his Word, we do so at our peril.

Hear me well. I do not advocate some kind of tight religion. Christianity is not morality—toeing the line and keeping the rules. Christianity is a relationship with God who loves you so much that he gave you his Son, and values you so much he has made you his child. God's every gift is good and perfect. He can never cast a shadow on your life by turning from his goodness. The essence of sin lies in doubting God's goodness and then rejecting his Word. The garden belongs to you as a gift from his hand. Enjoy it. Trust him.

Commentary

The account of the fall describes how, as Helmut Thielicke says, "evil streams out like an icy breath into the world, into a world that once was sound and whole, a world over which there rang the joy of the Creator: 'Behold, it was very good; behold it is very good.' "[1] While this episode comes to us like an epic out of the ancient past, all of us recognize in this account seductions as up-to-date as our most recent fall.

I preached this sermon at a chapel service for the students and faculty of Denver Seminary. While the message itself is as universal as sin, like any sermon, it was prepared and preached for a particular audience. Glimpses of those hearers flash throughout the message.

The sermon takes the form of a "subject completed." The subject gets restated three times in the introduction with three different questions which ask the same thing, "How does the tempter do his work? How does he come to us? How does he destroy us?" The sermon makes two basic observations about that subject.

1. Helmut Thielicke, *How the World Began: Man in the First Chapters of the Bible,* trans. John W. Doberstein (Philadelphia: Muhlenberg, 1961), p. 123.

> I. When Satan tempts us, he comes to us in disguise.
> A. He disguises his person.
> B. He disguises his purpose.
> II. When Satan tempts us, he levels his attack against God.
> A. He causes us to doubt God's Word.
> B. He causes us to distrust God's character.

The sermon, therefore, elaborates one central idea: "Satan comes to us in disguise to cause us to distrust God's character and to doubt God's Word." While it takes thirty minutes to say it, the sermon says no more than that. The purpose for preaching this sermon grows out of the idea: to help the listeners guard against the tempter by knowing his strategy of attack.

An introduction should do three things. First, it gains attention for the idea; second, it establishes need for what follows; and third, it orients the listeners to the body of the sermon.

The opening illustration, therefore, catches attention and establishes a need to listen to what follows. The story prompts the question, "If an effective Christian leader can end up in a penitentiary, who among us can assume we don't need to know how the enemy works?" In the third, fourth, and fifth paragraphs the sermon probes that need and relates it in a personal way both to the preacher and his hearers.

An introduction also does its work when it orients the congregation to the biblical passage and the body of the sermon. In doing that, it usually answers two questions: "Why are we turning to this particular passage today?" and "How will this sermon go about meeting the need that has been raised?" The sermon presents the account of the fall as "a case study of temptation," and the passage in Genesis governs the development. Both major points as well as the subpoints come out of the biblical account of the fall. The Bible is used throughout the sermon in other ways. An illustration of a minor point comes from the story of Ruth and Naomi, and another subpoint is reinforced by a series of warnings from other parts of the Scriptures.

The sermon is also personal. That note sounds not only in

COMMENTARY

24

the introduction but throughout the development. The pronouns *we, us, our, you,* and *your* are used frequently. The points are also stated in terms of the audience, not in terms of the passage in Genesis. Satan comes to us; he attacks us. An expository preacher trades a sword for a butter knife when he sounds like a lecturer in ancient history discussing a saga from the long ago and far away. Biblical preaching does not simply deal with the text; it talks about people from the text. Relevance is found in part when the minister speaks to the congregation as though the sermon was designed for them.

The wording of the sermon adds something to its basic thrust. Wording in a sermon must attack the barricades of a listener's inattention with ferocity. Language close to the senses peppers any relevant sermon: "Satan ... does not come in the form of a coiled snake" or "with the roar of a lion" or "with the wail of a siren" or "waving a red flag." While this sermon uses only two longer formal illustrations, it bristles with short one-line examples drawn from Faust, Shakespeare, modern advertising, motion pictures, television, and novels. Images flash into the mind with sentences like "once the well is poisoned, all the water is polluted" and "when Satan approaches us, he never comes dragging the chains that will enslave us."

The sermon has weaknesses. While the subject "How does the tempter do his work?" comes through clearly, the statement of the sermon's central idea does not. The transitions link the two major points to each other and the supporting points to their main points, but they do not clearly restate the subject or the big idea of the sermon.

The conclusion, too, could have had more strength. While "the essence of sin lies in doubting God's goodness and then rejecting his Word" restates the basic thrust of the message, the closing would possess more force had it been more specific and sharply focused. People need to know what to do with what they know and, if possible, they need clues as to how to do it immediately. The best conclusions provide that direction.

How long does it take you to put a sermon together?

My quick answer is eleven to twelve hours. If I kept a log of my time, like a lawyer accounting for every ten minutes I thought about a sermon, I suspect it would be longer.

How about this sermon? Did it take eleven to twelve hours?

I guess so. I preach regularly in our chapel here at Denver Seminary. I keep folders on messages I want to develop. Whenever I come across something in my reading or in my study of a passage, I put it in the folder. When I actually sit down to work through the sermon, it takes eight to ten hours, but I have a lot of work already done in the folder in front of me.

How long do you preach?

That varies from twenty-five minutes to forty minutes. It depends on the sermon and where I am preaching.

Where do you get ideas for your sermons?

Well, either you start with the Scriptures and go to people's needs, or you start with people's needs and go to the Bible. I usually start with a passage that has caught my attention and work from there. When I teach a businessmen's Bible study, I work through a book of the Bible or a section of a book. That's an advantage of consecutive exposition of the Scriptures. You know what you will preach next even if you may not know exactly what the text is saying when you come to it. Unfortunately, in my role as president of a seminary, I can't always do that when I speak.

Can you remember how this sermon came about?

I had been reading through Genesis and trying to understand how narrative literature in the Bible communicates its concepts. I found the opening chapters of Genesis intriguing and a bit puzzling. After all, you and I don't have much contact with talking serpents or gardens like Eden. Yet, behind these stories lies theology. I'm persuaded that the opening chapters of the Bible don't simply tell us how the world began or about primordial days. They transcend specific history. At any rate, I read *How the World Began* by Helmut Thielicke and I felt he provided a workable lead to the application of the passage. That was in my folder. I also had some notes from a lecture that my friend, Bruce Waltke, gave fifteen years ago. Finally, I was deeply bothered about the young pastor who ended up in a Texas prison. All of that drew me back to this chapter and that material.

How do you go about preparing your sermon?

First, I spend time in the text until I think I understand what the biblical author was saying to his readers. Why did he write this? What difference would it make were it not there? How does this account relate to the context that precedes it and follows it? I look for structural clues or clues in the narrative that open up the passage. The biblical writers were marvelous storytellers. They didn't simply spin yarns. They taught theology. I try to be aware of how they went about doing that.

What do you actually do? What lies before you on your desk?

I use a series of legal-size yellow pages; one page for each verse, or each paragraph, depending on the length of my passage. Any observation that comes to me from my study or reading that relates to a particular verse, I put there. I usually have a page to sketch an outline and to write down the subject of the passage and the complement. When I think I understand the passage, I feel a sense of relief. That is the first major aim of my study, to capture what the biblical writer is saying and why.

What do you do then?

Having that material in hand, I then ask myself, "What is the most effective way to communicate this message to men and women today?" To bridge the gap between the dynamics of the situation in the ancient world and where we live today, and to do that with integrity, is probably the most challenging part of preaching. Scholars have seldom given application the attention it deserves. So I try to ask how this passage speaks to me and to other people I know and then how I can best get it across. I try not to think about preaching a sermon, but how to communicate a biblical concept from the passage to my audience.

Where do you use commentaries?

Pretty early in the process. I use any help I can get to understand the text. I find, though, that I need to have the content of the passage in mind before I use the tools. Otherwise I don't know what the commentaries are talking about. I read the more technical material first.

What about illustrations? How important are they?

I think they are crucial. They plant truth in people's lives. Illustrations can explain an idea, help people see its validity, and understand what difference it makes in their lives.

You collect them?

Yes, collecting illustrations is my hobby. Other people collect postage stamps and baseball cards; I gather illustrations. I think the process is as important as the product. As you look for illustrations, it turns the world into God's picture book and stimulates your imaginative glands.

Where do you find your illustrations?

Everywhere. From my reading, of course. Magazines, books, newspapers, the comics. From conversations or something that strikes me in life that I think could be turned into an illustration. I steal them from other preachers as I listen to them or read their sermons.

What do you think is the weakest part of your own preaching?

For any given sermon, I might answer that differently. Sometimes I feel my conclusion needed more work, especially in showing people how to make the truth a part of their lives. At other times, I feel that the tension was weak or that the sermon was too long. Thinking of sermons as a group, I guess I fail in my transitions most often. I don't take time to build a bridge between my major points, to review or go back to my central idea. The sermon is clear to me as I preach it, and I assume it's also clear to the listeners. Listening to a sermon on tape three or four weeks later, I discover that the link between the points got lost in the preaching.

Does that discourage you?

Yes and no. Yes, in that you'd think if you teach homiletics, you'd get it right yourself, and I don't always. No—sermons are not literary masterpieces. They are living communication, and when you concentrate on getting something across to another person, there's a roughness to it. Battles for clarity never stay won and, while I strive to improve, I can't let reality defeat me or I'd never preach again.

Do you always preach without notes?

Yes, and we teach our students at Denver Seminary to do that. Research shows that a very limited amount of notes doesn't get in the way, but a couple of pages of notes hinders communication. So, I don't use them except for quotes or material like that.

How do you do that?

I think the secret lies in clear, full-sentence outlining. A preacher needs to "see" his flow of thought not as a series of individual points, but as a complete unit. If you know what you want to say and it hangs together logically or psychologically, then preaching resembles an animated conversation. If you're an expository preacher, the text often serves as "notes." After all, that's where you found the sermon. If a communicator trusts his or her mind, it's not that difficult and it adds to the directness of the sermon.

A final question. What advice would you give to a young minister?

You can't do better than Paul's counsel to Timothy. "Devote yourself to the public reading of Scripture, to preaching and to teaching." As you grow as a person, your sermons grow, too. But it's also crucial to grow as a preacher. As people see your progress, they will respect you and respond to your ministry.

Chapter 2

Thou Shalt Not Commit Adultery
Exodus 20:14

Erwin W. Lutzer

Erwin W. Lutzer is senior pastor of Moody Memorial
Church in Chicago. Books he has authored include
*Failure: The Back Door to Success, How in This World
Can I Be Holy?, Dorie: The Girl Nobody Loved,
Exploding the Myths That Could Destroy America,* and
Pastor to Pastor: Tackling Problems of the Pulpit.

In his book *The Myth of the Greener Grass* J. Allan Peterson tells the story of a woman who was at lunch with eleven other people. They had been studying French together while their children were in a nursery school. One woman asked the group, "How many of you have been faithful to your husbands throughout your marriage?" Only one woman at the table raised her hand.

That evening, this woman told her husband the story and added that she, herself, had not raised her hand.

"But I have been faithful," she assured him.

"Then why didn't you raise your hand?"

"I was ashamed."[1]

Ashamed of fidelity! In the past, the burden of shame fell on those who broke their vows but in our society, that has been changed. We've all seen television interviews of people who freely confess to having affairs. It seems to be the modern, so-phisticated thing to do. Only killjoys still believe in fidelity.

1. J. Allan Peterson, *The Myth of the Greener Grass* (Wheaton, Ill.: Tyndale, 1983), p. 17.

Pornography sends out a not-so-subtle message to our society: have as many relationships as you want, with anyone you want, just as long as they are pleasurable and "don't hurt anybody." Most of the sex in movies is not between married people. The impression given is those who live in the fast lane are the only ones who know what life is all about. Everyone else is out of step with society.

One man who writes scripts for television says that his goal is to get people to laugh at adultery, homosexuality, and incest. He says, "If you can get them to laugh at these things, it breaks down their resistance to them." One recent survey suggests that perhaps as many as one-half of all marriage partners, at some time or another, have an affair.

Yet, the seventh commandment says, "Thou shalt not commit adultery." Why did God give this command? Isn't this unrealistic, considering the strong sexual desire that all of us experience? But even in the twentieth century, there are some valid reasons why we should obey this command. Let's consider some of them.

First, we should not commit adultery because God says we shouldn't!

Already I can hear a chorus of objections to the idea that we should do something (or not do something) just "because God says so!" After all, we live in a day and age when everyone is educated and we should be able to make our own decisions on these matters. How can God saying, "No," make it wrong? Mark Twain railed in anger against a God who would give us such a strong sexual drive only to limit its expression to one person within the marriage bond.

But, of course, there was a reason why God gave this commandment. He created us in such a way that we are unable to have sex outside of marriage without guilt and emotional tension. Adultery destroys us on the inside; it brings about an inner death.

The Bible specifically teaches that the sex act joins two people together—body, soul, and spirit. "Do you not know that he who unites himself with a prostitute is one with her in body? For it is said, 'The two will become one flesh' " (1 Cor. 6:16). Even a casual relationship with a prostitute means that there is more than just the joining of two bodies. Sex is more than a biological act; there is an inner psychological bond that develops between two people during the sex act. When sex is practiced outside of the protection of a marriage covenant, there is inevitable hurt and the bruising of the emotions. Sexual immorality of all kinds is a blow aimed at the heart of self-respect and personhood.

I once counseled a sixteen-year-old woman who had been seduced by an older married man who was the father of several children. When the affair, which lasted several months, was discovered, he blamed it all on her. She had been led along by the sweet, deceptive words of this older man. Who can understand the rejection she felt when it all blew up, and he refused to take any responsibility for it? Yet, interestingly, she said, "That happened three years ago and I still can't get him out of my mind. I'd go to bed with him today if he were to ask me to." Why would this young woman still feel such an attachment to a man who had betrayed her? Psychologically, she was feeling the effects of the "one flesh" relationship. That's the nature of illicit sexuality.

Don't misunderstand: to have sex is not equivalent to marriage. Marriage is protected by a covenant; it involves a promise to live together "in sickness and in health till death do us part." The covenant constitutes the marriage, sex completes it. But when there is sex without a covenant, there is a psychological "joining together" of two people that has emotional repercussions. The result of such an affair is either guilt or a hardened conscience.

We've all met people who tell us that they have an affair that is both loving and caring. One woman told me that she lived with an alcoholic husband and if it wasn't for a relationship she had with another man, she would have lost her sanity. Another adulterer said, "I have found an oasis, and now you're telling me to go back to the desert."

There's no question that there can be loving adulterous relationships. People have often "found each other" and discover levels of communication that they've not had in their own marriages. Yes, some of these relationships are loving and meaningful. The problem is an adulterer has to break at least five of the Ten Commandments to have this "meaningful relationship."

Let's consider the commandments an adulterer breaks. The first says, "Thou shalt have no other gods before me." An adulterer says that there is a relationship that is more important than the relationship with God. What about the command, "Thou shalt not bear false witness"? An adulterer breaks his vow, and usually lies to cover his sin. Another commandment is "Thou shalt not steal." When David sinned with Bathsheba, Nathan the prophet basically said that he had stolen another man's wife. The last commandment says, "Thou shalt not covet." Adultery begins with a coveting heart. Finally, we return to the seventh commandment which says explicitly, "Thou shalt not commit adultery."

Perhaps now we can understand why adultery is such a serious sin. One must shake his fist in God's face in order to have the relationship. When God said, "Thou shalt not commit adultery," it was not because he was against sex, but because he believed sex was so good, he wanted to protect it from being misused.

For those who have been involved in sexual sin, there is hope. God can forgive the past, cleanse the conscience, and give the adulterer a new beginning. The scars may still be there, but the guilt and frustration will be gone. For the God who gave the command is the same God who is able to forgive.

Second, we should not commit adultery because of the consequences. Sexual sin is the most deceptive temptation we can face. It promises so much, but in the end is bitter. Our desires tell us that they must be fulfilled regardless of the cost. A popular song says, in effect, "I'll fulfill my passions today and deal with the devil tomorrow." We've all known people who have said they would have this relationship at any cost. One man said, "I'd rather go to hell with my mistress than to heaven with my wife."

What are the consequences that come to those participating in an adulterous relationship? First of all, there is an inner destruction, a feeling of guilt. No matter how well the sin is hidden, it is always accompanied by a nagging conscience. One girl, who was a virgin until the age of twenty-nine but became angry at God because he didn't give her a husband, had a relationship with a man she didn't even respect. After it was over, the words *Now you are defiled* came to mind, almost as if from Satan. Illicit relationships promise like a god, but pay like the devil. This explains why those who practice immorality are caught between conflicting emotions. On the one hand, there is exhilarating pleasure, but on the other, the nagging knowledge that one is living a lie. For some, the guilt is overwhelming. No matter how well the affair is concealed, no matter how many precautions are taken so that it will never be discovered, it always is there in the mind. When the telephone rings, the adulterer wonders, "Does someone know?" And when friends come for a visit, the adulterer wonders whether, perhaps, they know the secret. Even in the most holy moments, when an adulterer wants to worship God in church, the memory of his sin flashes through his mind. As David said, "My sin is always before me."

But there is also the outer destruction, the hurt when the affair is finally discovered. The sense of rejection experienced by the partner who has been betrayed and the mistrust that accompanies it are unbelievable. Many people find it difficult to regain their own sense of self-worth when they know that their partner has been cheating. In one sense, adultery is one of the most selfish sins. However gratifying it may be to the adulterer, to those around him and to his family in particular the hurt not only is deep, but it may last forever.

God gave this commandment for the stability of the family. Every child grows up wanting parents who love each other. There is nothing as debilitating in the life of a child than to know that his father has found someone more attractive. Recent studies indicate that children whose parents are divorced experience much more hurt than originally realized.

One day on a talk show, someone asked me, "Don't you think that someone whose wife is in a wheelchair, and therefore unable to have sexual relations . . . don't you think that in a case like that it would be all right for a man to have an affair?" The hidden presupposition behind this question is that our passions must be fulfilled at any cost. In our society, controlling passion is an unpardonable sin. Every sensual desire of the body that screams for gratification must be fulfilled.

No one can justify illicit sexuality. If you make exceptions for such a person, then what about singles, widows, and those that are divorced? Our passions lie—it is not true that they must always be fulfilled. There are thousands of Christians sitting in jail today because of their faith in Jesus Christ who have no opportunity for sexual intimacy with wives or husbands. Yet they manage even in the midst of such repressive circumstances. Henry Bowman said, "No really intelligent person will burn down a cathedral to fry an egg, even if he is ravenously hungry." The cathedral of marriage is so special, no one has the right to burn it down just because he happens to have met someone who fulfills his needs or is sexually attractive.

Ultimately, we are answerable to God. However much sin may be hidden, it will eventually be brought out into the open. "Marriage should be honored by all, and the marriage bed kept pure, for God will judge the adulterer and all the sexually immoral" (Heb. 13:4). One reason we should live in sexual purity is because it is the command of God. Second, there are bitter consequences that come to those who flaunt their freedom. And finally, there is the compensation that comes from successfully resisting temptation.

A blessed promise comes to those who resist sexual temptation. When speaking about lust, Christ said, "If your right eye causes you to sin, gouge it out and throw it away. It is better for you to lose one part of your body than for your whole body to be thrown into hell. And if your right hand causes you to sin, cut it off and throw it away. It is better for you to lose one part of your body than for your whole body to go into hell" (Matt. 5:29–30).

Christ here refers to the two parts of the body that are often involved in sexual arousal. The first is the eye which, particularly for men, causes sexual desire. The second is the hand; women are often stimulated with tender caresses. Jesus says in no uncertain terms: "Whatever you have to do to take away the stumbling blocks—do it!" It's worth it!

He says, "It is better." The handicapped person, with only one eye and one hand, is better off than the person who is whole but has attracted the displeasure of God. It is better to be sexually frustrated and lonely than to bear the scars of infidelity. The person who obeys the commandment retains his dignity and self-worth. He escapes the inner conflict and guilt associated with low-commitment sex. But more importantly, he keeps his fellowship with God. "Blessed are the pure in heart, for they will see God" (Matt. 5:8).

Sexual temptation gives us one of the clearest opportunities to prove our love for God. We're not asked to sacrifice our son on an altar as Abraham did (though God may take one of our children in death to test our faith). But there are other ways that God has of testing us—and for many, it is sexual temptation. At stake is whether we value our relationship with God more than we do the fulfillment of our own desires.

What about the person who has committed adultery in the past, or is involved in a relationship now? One of the most accurate barometers of the human heart is how we respond when sin is pointed out to us. There are many people who, when caught in adultery, simply tell one lie after another trying to hold on to their cover.

There was a man whose wife suspected that he was committing adultery, but she didn't have conclusive evidence. Yes, he admitted that he had been with another woman, that he had even been up to her apartment, but "they hadn't done anything." To prove it, he put his hand in the air and said, "If I'm lying, may God smite me dead."

But lying he was! Later, he was forced to admit that he had indeed put God to the test—if the Lord had taken him up on that oath, he would have died in his tracks. Yet, for all that, when I asked his wife whether or not he asked for her forgiveness, she said, "Well, sort of. . . ." In a roundabout way, he said he was sorry, but he still wouldn't face his sin directly.

That's hardheartedness! It's one thing to sin; it's quite another to keep justifying yourself once it is pointed out. Peter and Judas both denied Christ. One repented and the other refused to face his sin and committed suicide.

David eventually confessed his sin, but it took several months before he stopped pretending. Eventually, he was able to say, "Blessed is he whose transgressions are forgiven, whose sins are covered. Blessed is the man whose sin the LORD does not count against him, and in whose spirit there is no deceit" (Ps. 32:1)

God gave us the commandment "Thou shalt not commit adultery." We should never be ashamed of believing that he knows best. And with the command comes the divine enablement to live up to this standard. Blessed are those who are not ashamed to obey his Word.

SERMON

40

While biblical sermons usually deal with a paragraph or several paragraphs of Scripture, this sermon focuses on a single verse from the Ten Commandments: "Thou shalt not commit adultery." It is one of a series of messages Erwin Lutzer preached on the Decalogue.

The sermon is a "proposition proved." In the introduction the preacher sets this commandment up against the prevailing attitudes of our society and then asks, "Isn't this unrealistic, considering the strong sexual desire that all of us experience?" In other words, he raises the functional question, "Is this true? Should I believe it?" The sermon then takes the form of proofs for the statement, "Thou shalt not commit adultery." The big idea stands like a proposition in a debate. The reasons supporting the proposition emerge clearly.

I. We should not commit adultery because it is against God's command.
   A. The Bible says that the sex act joins two people together, body, soul, and spirit (1 Cor. 6:16).

B. An adulterer breaks at least five of the Ten Commandments.

  II. We should not commit adultery because of the consequences of an adulterous relationship.

A. One consequence lies within us (Ps. 51:3).

B. Another consequence lies outside us.

  III. We should not commit adultery because of the compensation for fidelity (Matt. 5:8).

In every sermon he preaches, Lutzer uses a key word, a plural noun that groups his ideas, to achieve parallelism in his points and centrality of purpose for his sermon. In this sermon his key word is "reasons" and his major points are alliterated "The Command of God," "The Consequences," and "The Compensation for Fidelity." The development is clear and easy to follow and that stands as a major strength of the sermon. While the statement of the points contains the common letter *c,* the points are not stated in parallel fashion. The advantage of alliteration is that it provides a hook for the memory. The danger comes when the foot is altered to fit the shoe.

The sermon is relevant. When the flint of people's questions strikes the steel of the Word of God, a spark emerges that makes a sermon glow. The twentieth-century outline and the content of this message are as up-to-date as tomorrow's soap opera or the surgeon general's campaign against AIDS. Five specific examples of sexual encounters between particular men and women fix the sermon firmly in life. Lutzer's other supporting material comes from pornography, television, a talk show, a pop song, and surveys and stories drawn from American society.

The sermon also reflects an awareness of the listeners. Lutzer sits with his audience by using phrases such as "We've all seen...," "We've all met people who...," "We've all known...." In addition he anticipates reactions from his congregation. "Already I can hear a chorus of objections...," "Someone asked me...," "What about the person who has committed adultery in the past?..." An effective communicator keeps his hearers in mind when he prepares his sermon as he preaches.

Exegetes and some homileticians will ask an important question of definition: "Can a sermon based on a single verse qualify as exposition?" A great deal depends on the text and how the sermon develops. When the sentence treated lies within a broader passage—for example, John 3:16 which is a fragment of Jesus' larger conversation with Nicodemus—then the sermon can be expository if it derives its content and development from the wider context of thought. A sermon cannot be called expository which merely tips the hat to the context or ignores it completely and uses the single verse as a launching pad for the preacher's own thought.

Some verses, however, stand alone. That is true, for instance, of many of the proverbs or, as here, each one of the Ten Commandments. The immediate context of Exodus 20 does not elaborate on the commands; therefore, the minister must wrestle with why God makes the prohibition. A biblical sermon, however, first looks at whether the Scriptures speak to this command in any other place and then works with that material to develop the thought. Lutzer summons Paul, David, Jesus, and the commandments themselves as well as examples from life today to support his reasons for the command against sexual looseness. The verse, then, becomes the focal point of a concept dealt with extensively throughout the rest of the Bible. In the final analysis, a sermon is biblical if the substance of its thought comes directly from the Scriptures. It is expository when the passages chosen govern the development of the entire sermon or its individual points. There is no doubt that this particular sermon reflects the teaching of Scripture, but in the strictest sense it is not expository.

A sermon based on a negative text can produce a negative sermon. While Lutzer preaches from the Law, he also preaches grace and hope. His conclusion sounds a positive note and offers some direction to men and women who desire to change their attitudes and behavior.

COMMENTARY

43

How long does it usually take you to prepare a message?

About six to eight hours.

How long did it take you to prepare the message you submitted?

About six to eight hours.

How long are your sermons normally?

Almost thirty minutes exactly. I don't preach it ahead of time, but I must have an internal clock—which is good for our radio program.

How do you go about preparing your sermons?

I read the text or the passage. If I'm preaching through Romans, I'm constantly reading Romans and trying to understand Paul's argument. If I'm in Psalms, I read those psalms until I find out the "bottom line" or the central idea of what I want to communicate. Once I've done that, I usually go ahead and make up my outline.

To what extent do you use commentaries or the original language?

Usually it is *after* I make the outline. I go to commentaries and critical works to understand the text more clearly. In the process of doing that, I may change my outline. But usually I work with the English text until I have a satisfactory outline and then I'll do whatever study is necessary to substantiate those points and to make sure that I'm biblical.

Do you always use commentaries?

For some messages I've preached I didn't consult a commentary. There are other passages, especially in the Old Testament (like Psalms), where I have to consult commentaries. Some expressions may not be clear and I keep asking, "What is the psalmist saying here?" I go through the psalm very carefully so that I understand the wording and the phrases. On the other hand, if I'm preaching a narrative section, I may not use any exegetical works because the content is so evident.

How do you keep track of your materials as you study?

Once I have my outline, I will write the first point on top of one page and a second point on top of another page. I fill in the content from my study that substantiates, clarifies, or relates to each specific point.

Are there other helps you use?

Whenever possible, I like to read a sermon or two that somebody else has preached on that text. It is amazing how other men's insights trigger all kinds of illustrations or ideas as to how a text may be developed. I may actually use a point from someone's sermon because it strikes me with such force. I've sometimes approached a text without enthusiasm, and then I've read what someone else has said about it, and that has been a catalyst to get me fired up and say, "This is an explosive passage."

Any particular commentaries or preachers that stir you?

I like to read Campbell Morgan and Lidden. MacLaren is very profitable for illustrations and development. Often I read a sermon by Spurgeon.

Where do you get your illustrations?

Everywhere I can. I have illustration books, and I use them. I have illustration files. In the process of reading other people's sermons, I get illustrations. If I hear a good one, I write it down and throw it into a file that I have here. It's the old story: you beg, you borrow, and you steal. You get them from wherever you possibly can, but whatever you do, you get them because they are incredibly important to preaching.

How do you develop introductions to your sermons?

First, the introduction should introduce the subject! Generally, I introduce that subject by raising a felt need. I try to get a feel for my audience and try to think of what they have come through. I preached on anxiety recently. It's very easy to paint pictures of what each of us goes through with the pressures of life. I am constantly thinking in terms of where people are. Then I usually raise a problem or make a general observation or ask a question. In some way I begin with the audience rather than the text. I normally try to tie the conclusion with the introduction. That's a characteristic of good writing as well as good preaching. If you begin with a topic and end with that very same idea, maybe even repeating a phrase, there's something within people that says, "He knew where he began and he knew where he was going and he knew where he ended." It brings a sense of unity to the sermon.

You preached this sermon on a single sentence. What particular challenges does that present?

Whenever you preach on the Ten Commandments, the greatest challenge is to discover what direction you are going to take with each of them. Each one is only a phrase or a line. You have to ask yourself, "What am I going to do with this phrase?" In this case, I asked the question, "Why did God give this command," or "Why is God opposed to adultery?" That's also in the minds of people.

Why did you shape the sermon as you did?

The average person says to himself, "Why does God give that commandment? Here I am with my sexual desires, here is the availability of a beautiful partner, and my marriage is on the rocks. Why shouldn't I?" I thought about what the people were thinking and I developed it from there.

Any particular problems in preaching on the Ten Commandments?

The preacher must be aware of the Old Testament background out of which these commandments were given. One must also think through the relevance of the commandments to the New Testament era and to today. A dispensationalist is going to handle them differently from a covenant theologian.

Do you always use a key word in organizing your sermons?

Yes, there are two reasons for this: (1) because it immediately achieves parallelism, and (2) because when I use the transitional sentence to get into the body of the sermon, people all over the audience look for scraps of paper and take out their pens to take notes.

Doesn't this technique limit your variety?

I think that developing ideas around a key word never limits one's variety. After all, there are hundreds of key words. You can have four "barriers" to effective prayer. That's as different from three "reasons" why you should not commit adultery as day is from night. The structure may be the same in the sense that you have a key word, but the content is different.

You've come a long way since you sat in a class in homiletics. I'm sure you've thrown away a lot of chaff. Did you find any wheat?

Without question, the most helpful thing was the emphasis on getting a single idea. A second thing I still remember is that a sermon should have unity, order, and progress. A sermon should go somewhere. If you were to cut me off in the middle of a sermon, people would realize that the sermon was not completed. It would be clear that I had not yet arrived at my destination. That means I spend a lot of time working on my conclusions. I think they are essential. Many relatively poor sermons have been salvaged by a strong conclusion. I never leave the conclusion to chance. Third, I am aware of my audience. It doesn't matter how well I preach if nobody listens. Knowing your congregation is absolutely essential to good preaching.

Do you have any further observations about preparation?

The preparation of the preacher's heart is as important as the preparation of his sermon. Perhaps the same amount of time that goes into the preparation of the sermon ought to go into the preparation of the preacher's heart. I need the work of the Holy Spirit, and I think personally that in the last four or five months God has given me a greater liberty to preach. I'm spending much more time in prayer and in submission and in preparation of my heart.

How would someone begin to do this?

Every preacher, if he's honest, comes to a point where he begins to admit to himself that his sermons are not doing nearly as much good as he thinks they should. I came to that point. That makes one very honest before God, and very helpless before God. It brings a level of submission to God and a dependency that a naturally gifted person doing well in the ministry may not seek out because he is doing so well. You tend to say, "Well, I know I can do it." But the real question is, "Do I do it in the fullness and in the power of the Holy Spirit with a burning heart?" One can't take that for granted. I think this comes only when one is honest enough to see the shallowness of preaching any other way.

Chapter 3

The Big Valley
1 Samuel 17:1–51

James O. Rose

James O. Rose presently is senior pastor of Calvary Baptist Church in New York City. Prior to this, he served churches in Connecticut, Texas, and Florida. Jim's tapes of sermons and "how-to" tapes on preparing dramatic presentations have a national and international distribution. Jim has written articles for various magazines and journals. He speaks regularly at pastors' conferences, in churches, and in the Far East, India, and Europe. Jim and his wife, Phyllis Ann, often speak at Bible conferences and in Family Life series. Jim speaks regularly on university campuses.

The stillness of early morning was reinforced by the mist filling the floor of a sprawling valley. It is like that in spring; it's the time of green grass and gorgeous wildflowers. It's the time of gentle warmth and it is the time of going out to war. On this morning men are moving in silence out to the very lip of the great valley, called Elah. Some are shoving the last few bits of bread and cheese into their mouths. Others are adjusting their spears, slings, and war gear. Now all are finally in place; again there is eerie silence.

In the middle of the attack line an officer raises his arm and at the signal, the army of Israel shouts, *"Ruah,"* their war cry. From the other side of the valley, there should come a response from the Philistines. After all, they had initiated this conflict. These same Philistines had been beaten badly at Michmash in their last outing, beaten by this same army of ignorant Hebrew farmers. The Philistines were a big power. They had to put these farmers in their places before they got too big for their political britches. But where were the Philistines on this morning? There was something going on over on the Philistine side; it sounded like a tank rumbling into place, except they didn't have tanks.

Yes, there is definitely movement down on the valley floor. As the breeze pushes the mist aside, murmuring breaks out down among the Israelites. "It's a big rock! No, it's a tree. No, it moves!" A roar from the valley floor removes all questions. "It's a man!" Still no one moves, and can you blame them?

> A champion named Goliath, who was from Gath, came out of the Philistine camp. He was over nine feet tall. He had a bronze helmet on his head and wore a coat of scale armor of bronze weighing five thousand shekels; on his legs he wore bronze greaves, and a bronze javelin was slung on his back. His spear shaft was like a weaver's rod, and its iron point weighed six hundred shekels. His shield bearer went ahead of him. (1 Sam. 17:4–7)

SERMON

54

He's nine foot six! This human tank is wearing a bronze shirt that weighs one hundred twenty-six pounds and the head of his spear alone weighs nineteen pounds. (An Olympic shotput weighs only sixteen pounds.) He's a man . . . with a message, a challenge to single combat. This ugly giant is a real threat, and Israel's petrified! Not to worry: they have Saul! Saul's also big, head and shoulders bigger than everyone else in Israel. "Saul, that's your kind of challenge. Saul, hey, Saul. . . ." Israel is retreating, running. It's a rout and Saul is running with the rest.

The problem? Saul, God's first king-elect, is on his own now. He wanted it that way and now he's got it. God has left him. Did I say on his own? Not completely. When someone has tasted God's opportunities and turns away, the Lord lifts the energy shield and the other side sends in a discomforter.

Saul is looking at life from ground level. Giants are overwhelming to those who look at life from that level. Giants are terribly hard to handle on your own. Israel ought to know: they've had giant troubles before. The report of Goliath's imposing ancestors stopped a whole generation of Israel at the door to the Promised Land. When the new crew finally did enter the Promised Land, only Caleb invaded giant country. He handled most of them, but at eighty years of age, we wouldn't expect him to get them all. Goliath is a leftover, a big leftover. And it only takes one giant leftover to unglue folks looking at life from ground level. From ground level giants fill up our screen. The closer we get, the bigger they look. We shouldn't consider giants unusual or unexpected. They roam in every generation—theirs at 1000 B.C. in Elah Valley and ours at A.D. 2000 in our valleys. I'll bet you've got one in your valley, a valley you must cross, if you're going on with God. I do, too. My giant has been waving at me lately.

The issue is: What are we going to do about our giants? Those locked into ground-level living refuse to face them. Goliath is down there day after day, and there's no getting around him. Still Israel has all but ignored him.

Without God, facing giants is impossible, and God is no longer with Saul. God, however, is still with Israel; he has moved into David's life. We remember David—king-elect, farmhand, shepherd. He's still tending sheep—although he has been able to spend a bit of time at the palace.

SERMON

55

> So Saul said to his attendants, "Find someone who plays well and bring him to me."
> One of the servants answered, "I have seen a son of Jesse of Bethlehem who knows how to play the harp. He is a brave man and a warrior. He speaks well and is a fine-looking man. And the LORD is with him."
> Then Saul sent messengers to Jesse and said, "Send me your son David, who is with the sheep." (1 Sam. 16:17–19)

Even if his family ignored David, others have noticed. So he came to the court, a singer and Saul's armor bearer.

Actually that wasn't such a big deal. It was more like going to West Point, Annapolis, or the Air Force Academy. Saul had lots of armor bearers. If you were to become an officer, that's the way you did it. David would do whatever armor bearers did and then play his harp and then he would go back for flock duty. In fact, David was back at the ranch when Goliath started his taunts. David probably wouldn't have gotten to go to battle as a soldier anyway. Junior armor bearers usually weren't invited to the big battles. He goes to battle, not as a warrior, but as a grocery boy. "Now Jesse said to his son David, 'Take this ephah of roasted grain and these ten loaves of bread for your brothers and hurry to their camp. Take along these ten cheeses to the commander of their unit. See how your brothers are and bring back some assurance from them' " (vv. 17–18). David doesn't get any respect at home either; he's still the insignificant one. Jesse even doubts he can deliver groceries. At least it was a break from watching the sheep and he could sneak a peek at the war.

David arrives just as the army is moving into attack position and just as they are shouting the *"ruah,"* although I suspect the *"ruah"* is like cheering when you're behind 55 to zip at half time.

As he has done every day for forty days, Goliath trudges down, shouting his challenge and with a yawn, waits. That is all it takes to turn Israel's line of skirmishers into a mob of soldiers, sprinting in the wrong direction.

Doesn't something strike you as strange about this? For forty days Israel has done the same thing. They prepare to fight a conventional war and scatter when Goliath shows up. The problem? They fail to deal with the real problem of confronting the giant in their valley. It's amazing how we deal so often with every problem but the real one, the one which takes God to resolve. Looking at life from the ground level causes you and me to ignore the giants, the giants God has equipped us to defeat by depending on him. Our marriage is struggling, but instead of trusting and correcting the problem, we increase our activities— joining another Bible study, taking up karate, and so on. God has given us giants to force us to look at life from his level. When we ignore the giants, godly living comes to a grinding halt. So it is with Israel's officers. Every night they gather in Saul's tent around the planning table and decide on the same strategy that ignores Goliath. They probably even pray about it. Then someone adds, "And God, get rid of that giant! He is ruining our strategy," at which point "amens" are heard throughout the tent. Yet on the fortieth day Israel is still doing the retreat shuffle. But on this day a startling thing happens in Elah Valley. David, the farmhand, the shepherd, stops running!

All of this happens as David is conversing with some soldiers in the rear of the ranks. When Goliath roars, David must have asked, "Why the retreat?" (vv. 24–25). "The one who fights him gets the king's daughter and money . . . and doesn't have to pay taxes," someone comments. "I'm already married and money is a curse and I love paying taxes and . . . have you seen Goliath?" No, David hasn't. But then David has never been bothered by gigantic obstacles. Sure, he's interested in what Saul has to offer. What has he ever gotten at home? He was probably ten years old before he knew his name wasn't "shut up," which in biblical language is "hold your peace." That's only a minor part of David's dynamic. The real fire that ignites his fuse can be found in his response: "Who is this uncircumcised Philistine that he should defy the armies of the living God?" (v. 26).

David, whose heart decides issues according to God's plan, sees life from God's perspective. David has a different way of looking at things. Israel and Saul are ground-level lookers, but David is, first and last, a man who looks at life from God's level. His mental screen is filled by the Lord, which makes every problem small in comparison. What ignites David on this day is Goliath blocking the plan and path of God. Those of us who see life from God's level, like David, are ignited into action by the giants that block the path of God.

It was my first year out of seminary in my first church and we weren't even being paid regularly. Giants were everywhere. Money was tight. Still Phyllis Ann and I saved enough for me to go to a pastors' conference. In one of the messages, the speaker stated something that refocused my life. "We," he said, "are all faced with a series of great opportunities brilliantly disguised as impossible problems." What was an impossible problem to Saul was a great opportunity for David.

David's determination to solve the problem impresses everyone, except David's brother Eliab, a sergeant in Saul's army. After all, what could a cadet know! When Eliab, David's oldest brother, heard him speaking with the men, he burned with anger at him and asked, 'Why have you come down here? And with whom did you leave those few sheep in the desert? I know how conceited you are and how wicked your heart is; you came down only to watch the battle.' 'Now what have I done?' said David. 'Can't I even speak?' " (vv. 28–29). This is an expanded version of "shut up!" The word does get out and around, however—all the way around to Saul.

> What David said was overheard and reported to Saul, and Saul sent for him.
>
> David said to Saul, "Let no one lose heart on account of this Philistine; your servant will go and fight him."
>
> Saul replied, "You are not able to go out against this Philistine and fight him; you are only a boy, and he has been a fighting man from his youth."
>
> But David said to Saul, "Your servant has been keeping his father's sheep. When a lion or a bear came and carried off a sheep from the flock, I went after it, struck it and rescued the sheep from its mouth. When it turned on me, I seized it by its hair, struck it and killed it. Your servant killed both the lion and the bear; this uncircumcised Philistine will be like one of them, because he has defied the armies of the living God. The LORD who delivered me from the paw of the lion and the paw of the bear will deliver me from the hand of this Philistine."
>
> Saul said to David, "Go, and the LORD be with you." (1 Sam. 17:31–37)

Saul, who knows there's no human way around Goliath, sends for David and is finally convinced the young man (a better rendering of the word of the text would be "youth") might have a chance. From David's answer Saul senses something of what had been, but was gone forever. To David Goliath would be like the lions and bears who bother the flock. These were, in David's view, actually attacking God. When our lives are lived for God's glory and great plan, those attacking us, those in our path, are actually attacking God; they are blocking his plan. David could go after lions, bears, or giants with the same conviction; God was working through him to remove obstacles. Giants in my valley and yours are in God's right-of-way, if we are living to do his will and looking at life from his level.

Well, Saul is convinced, but then it isn't hard to convince Saul with Goliath breathing down his neck. Rejecting Saul's armor, not because it is too big, but because he has never worn armor, David gets ready for Goliath. Saul's armor would not be too heavy for a man who could swing Goliath's sword. David does, however, get ready for Goliath in another way. God works that way; he works through us where we are with what we know to destroy the giants we face. David is at slingshot level (v. 40). Of course the sling in David's hand was lethal. It was the early version of the machine pistol with a five-shot clip.

The time has come. David steps out of the perimeter, where suddenly he is, by himself, against Goliath. One fall, winner takes all. He just pushes out; giants were always God's open doors. But the closer he gets, the bigger Goliath looks. Goliath is really bored by now; he wants his captain to signal a return. "Why, what's that kid doing out there? Looking for souvenirs? No, he's coming. No!" He's challenging "the Philistine." " 'Am I a dog, that you come at me with sticks?' " (v. 43). While part of single combat was yelling slogans at each other, David's response is a bit out of the ordinary.

> David said to the Philistine, "You come against me with sword and spear and javelin, but I come against you in the name of the LORD Almighty, the God of the armies of Israel, whom you have defied. This day the LORD will hand you over to me, and I'll strike you down and cut off your head. Today I will give the carcasses of the Philistine army to the birds of the air and the beasts of the earth, and the whole world will know that there is a God in Israel. All those gathered here will know that it is not by the sword or spear that the LORD saves; for the battle is the LORD's, and he will give all of you into our hands." (1 Sam. 17:45–47)

Watch out, big fellow! You see, Goliath, you are facing God today, and his plan is to let the earth know who he is. Sorry, but David's going to lay your body down! "As the Philistine moved closer to attack him, David ran quickly toward the battle line to meet him. Reaching into his bag and taking out a stone, he slung it and struck the Philistine on the forehead. The stone sank into his forehead, and he fell facedown on the ground." Like a quarterback on a roll-out, David darts to one side and with a move that's a blur, draws and throws. Zing! "Kid, I'm not moving until . . ." and the world goes black for Goliath. "So David triumphed over the Philistine with a sling and a stone; without a sword in his hand he struck down the Philistine and killed him. David ran and stood over him. He took hold of the Philistine's sword and drew it from the scabbard. After he killed him, he cut off his head with the sword. When the Philistines saw that their hero was dead, they turned and ran" (vv. 50–51). It is over, just that quickly. The Philistines have fled. Israel and Saul have won.

David sits exhausted and exhilarated by it all. What a day! He had arrived that morning a nameless errand boy, delivering groceries. Now as the sun is setting, he is the champion of Israel. It happens that way with those who see life from God's level. David, the boy with the sheep, is gone forever. David, the man of blood, the warrior, king-elect, has taken his place.

From childhood on we beg, "Tell me a story." In the world outside the church, ideas are wrapped up in stories. Novels, movies, and television do more to shape American thinking and values than scholarly position papers. The mini-drama in the sixty-second commercial moves the merchandise. When God communicated himself through the Bible, it is not surprising that he often used narratives about events and people. Robert Alter, in *The Art of Biblical Narrative,* argues that Old Testament authors were such skillful storytellers that what they wrote was really "fictionalized history" or "historical fiction."[1] We do not have to accept that verdict to agree that the biblical writers were skilled storytellers. Preachers true to the Scriptures and aware of their audiences also know the attractiveness of a story. Jim Rose turns into a storyteller in this message from 1 Samuel, one of a series of sermons he preached on the life of David.

Narrative sermons often prove difficult to outline. Transitions, points and subpoints, introductions and conclusions

1. Robert Alter, *The Art of Biblical Narrative* (New York: Basic Books, 1981).

simply do not play the part in narratives that they do in traditional sermons. Then too, most narratives develop inductively rather than deductively so that the idea emerges gradually
near the conclusion. That is true of this sermon. It makes two
major points and the second point also serves as the big idea
that generated the sermon.

    I. Giants threaten those of us who look at life from the
       ground level (1 Sam. 17:1–25).
       A. Those living with ground-level perspective are over-
          whelmed by giants.
       B. Those living with ground-level perspective refuse to
          face giants.
   II. Giants ignite those of us who look at life from a "God-
       level" perspective (1 Sam. 17:26–58).
       A. Giants look like great opportunities to those with a
          "God-level" perspective.
       B. Giant obstacles are open doors to those living with
          a "God-level" perspective.

While there are many different ways to tell a story, Jim Rose
chooses to work with this incident as a third-person narrator
recounting the events. While he seems to do little more than
relate the events and fill in some background, Rose obviously
had to work through the passage, understand its place in
1 Samuel, capture the historical background, and then stage
that material in the theater of his mind. Although story sermons sound simple, the art is concealed. When done creatively
and with integrity, they demand study and thought.

Stories hold their magnetic appeal because they stay close
to the way we learn best. While most classroom teaching and
much preaching is deductive—the lesson is stated, explained,
proved, and applied—life teaches us inductively as we live it.
We learn our deepest lessons through experience when we
smell, see, touch, hear, and feel for ourselves. Life is not an
abstraction.

A storyteller uses words to stimulate the senses. Rose uses

many: "stillness" (sound), "mist filling" (sight and touch), "moving in silence" (sight and sound), "tank rumbling" (sight and sound). His word choice brings David's battle into the twentieth century. "Tank rumbling," "human tank," "Olympic shotput," "like cheering when you're behind 55 to zip at half time," draw from our experiences which relate the past to the present. Both humor and human interest in the sermon come from seeing, hearing, and reacting to the appearance of Goliath while he taunts the Israelites from a distance. " 'It's a big rock! No, it's a tree. No, it moves!' A roar from the valley floor removes all questions. 'It's a man!' " To preach this sermon, Rose not only had to understand the story; he had to experience it. Then out of his imagination he selected the words that recreated that experience for his congregation.

While a preacher must rely on research and creativity to present a biblical narrative, much is also demanded of the congregation. The people in the pew must relate that message to their experience. Rose merely hints at how the biblical account relates to life today. "We are all faced with a series of opportunities brilliantly disguised as impossible problems," he warns us, but he doesn't display a rogue's gallery of problems that might prey upon us. The sermon ends when the story ends without a formal conclusion or appeal. Application in this sermon, therefore, is indirect and the hearers must fill in the blanks for themselves. Is that sufficient? Can a listener identify a "giant" in her life that needs conquering? Should the preacher say more? If so, what? When does a conclusion added to a story sound like a religious commercial? All of these questions arise as we weigh the strengths or weaknesses of a narrative sermon.

How long does it usually take you to prepare a message?

The genesis of a message starts a year before I preach it. I put together a sermon calendar for that year (I take a week off and put this together, including sermon titles, big ideas, and the chunk of Scripture for each sermon). Then I center my devotions on what I'll be preaching on a year from that date. At the most, I put in two hours per chapter then. A week and a half before I give the actual message, I pull out what I've done. I keep all of the material that I've been collecting for that sermon in a file. I usually spend an hour just looking over this material. The week of the message I put in seventeen to twenty-two hours on a sermon. This depends, of course, on the individual message.

How long are your sermons?

My messages normally will take from thirty to forty minutes. Narratives tend to be just a little longer.

How do you develop the biblical content of your sermons? To what extent do you use commentaries, original languages, Bible dictionaries, and so on?

That depends on the passage. I always translate the passage. In the New Testament I work only with the Greek text. Then I start thinking about the organization of the passage, how it flows. That is the hardest part. What is this author saying? How is he putting it together? The next thing I do when dealing with a New Testament passage is to go back to word studies or grammatical elements that need some work.

Where do you go from there?

I come up with an exegetical outline. This is an outline of the text as the author gave it, paraphrasing his thought. On Wednesday, I read commentaries about the passage a good bit. I work with the lexicon, with dictionaries, with encyclopedias, or look up the geography. After that, I develop a homiletical outline. This relates my study directly to the audience. Then I draw in illustrative material. Doing a sermon calendar one year in advance allows me to keep gathering illustrations. On Thursday I write out an abbreviated manuscript on all my previous study. That will come out about half or 40 percent in length of what the final manuscript will be. This helps me see the movement and connection and direction of the sermon. On Friday I manuscript the message. Saturday, I internalize it. I don't memorize it, but internalize it. And Sunday, I preach it.

Where do you get your illustrations?

From *U.S. News and World Report, Harper's, Atlantic Monthly,* the *Oxford Review.* Also, from the newspaper. I try to read a variety of books. Also, I pick up illustrations when I'm traveling. People send me articles or anecdotes they have enjoyed.

You use word pictures throughout your sermon. How do you come up with them?

They come naturally, I guess, but I also work at them. If I could get away with it, I'd do all narrative sermons because the illustrative material lies more in painting the picture with words. If a person doesn't work at it, even if words come easily, he may paint only with the same hues.

How do you develop introductions to your sermons?

The trap in introductions is that we gain interest but we don't connect. An introduction has to grab attention, but then it must direct that attention to what you're trying to communicate. In narrative messages, I'll usually try to start with a narrative introduction. I will try to paint a scene that has drama and leads into the passage. Second, variety is the key. Don't jump out from behind the same tree every week. Some weeks I'll use a visual for an introduction; I may use an illustration from life; or something right out of the morning paper. I may plant someone in the audience to ask a question. I may show the congregation a slide or a picture.

What do you think is the secret to effective narrative preaching?

Putting the narrative in present-day terminology. That makes its own application. I consciously try to repeat more in a narrative than I do in a didactic sermon. I find it necessary to repeat again and again, because people get lost in the story. If I don't repeat, they may have heard a good story, but it won't stick in their minds.

Your sermon on 1 Samuel 17 ends assuming that the audience will personally apply the message. Did you do this deliberately?

Let me explain the "response for life" time in our church. The response is a reflection on the application for today. I will literally step to a different point on the platform and say, "This is what we can do with this." I want people to know how this affects them in their world. This time is never over three minutes. I want to nail the big idea and try to relate it to the audience. I always have one after a narrative, and all my messages generally have a response. The narrative will, of course, have more detail. The first-person drama is the most difficult sermon to follow with a response time. Actually, it's usually more effective to have someone else do it.

You've been out of seminary for two decades now. What has lingered on from your homiletics classes?

First, the conviction that preaching is a tremendously effective tool to help people to grow up in Christ. Second, I have learned the importance of preaching one main idea. Third, I have come to appreciate the power of words. They are like barbs which catch in people's consciousness.

Chapter 4

A Night in Persia
Esther

Donald Sunukjian

Donald Sunukjian is currently the pastor of Westlake Bible Church in Austin, Texas. He served as associate professor at Dallas Theological Seminary from 1979 to 1988. Sunukjian's articles have appeared in *Bibliotheca Sacra, Kindred Spirit, Walvoord: A Tribute,* and the *Bible Knowledge Commentary.*

There's a book in the Bible where the name of God is never mentioned—the Book of Esther. But even though God's name is mentioned nowhere in the book, you sense his presence everywhere, controlling what happens.

It's like a dollhouse where the top has been removed and some big father can lean in, move the people around, rearrange the furniture, and do anything he wants. That huge father does not walk around in the dollhouse, yet he controls everything that happens. That's how it is in the Book of Esther. You don't see or hear God there, but you sense his presence dominating everything.

I would like to tell the story of Esther through the eyes of one of the minor characters of the book. The man is on the palace staff, an attendant to the king. He's on the inside. He knows everything that's going on. How would this man, who never hears the name of God and yet sees everything that happens, view it? What sense would he make out of it all?

My name is Harbona. My job? In Britain I would be called a personal valet. In your country I would be known as a male private secretary. In my country I am Harbona, chamberlain to Xerxes, king of Persia. You may know him by the name *Ahasuerus*. At first I hesitated to take the job because you never knew about Xerxes. One day you'd be good friends with him—everything would be great—and then all of a sudden, without warning, he'd turn on you and it was all over.

For instance, once Pythius, one of his leading officials, offered Xerxes four million dollars to pay for one of the Persian military campaigns. Xerxes was so overwhelmed by such generosity that he refused the money and even gave Pythius a present besides. But then a little later when Pythius hinted that maybe his oldest son could be excused from the campaign, Xerxes was so infuriated, he hacked the boy in two and marched his army between the pieces. That's what I mean when I say you never knew about Xerxes. Another time a storm at sea destroyed three hundred of his ships. Xerxes grabbed a strap, went down to the seashore, and beat the sea three hundred times, once for each ship.

So you can see why I hesitated to take the job. But I took it. I made up my mind that I would get along with Xerxes. I would never rub him the wrong way; I'd just "go with the flow."

But let me tell you about a series of amazing coincidences that have happened in Persia lately. It all began years ago after the Bay of Salamis fiasco. Real tragic. Xerxes was making a bid to take over Greece to expand the Persian Empire. He was doing well, too, until in one naval battle at the Bay of Salamis, his entire navy was wiped out and Xerxes had to sneak back to Persia on a fishing boat. For the longest time after that he was down in the dumps. He brooded all day long—no spark, no interest.

Then he started talking about Vashti: poor Vashti, how he'd done her wrong. I'll admit it had been an unfortunate affair. Vashti was the queen he had gotten rid of. But what's past is past. It wouldn't do any good to mope about it. I thought to myself, *Something's got to be done to put some life back into Xerxes. I know: women, and lots of them. That'll get his mind off Vashti.* So I told him my idea. "Xerxes, why don't you gather beautiful young virgins from all over the kingdom here in the palace? You can get to know them, and maybe you'll find one you like well enough to make a new queen." He went for the idea. It wasn't long before we had the best-looking girls in all Persia right here at the palace. The whole thing did wonders for Xerxes. All those pretty girls—he saw them all.

But there was one in particular who caught his eye. He began to see more and more of her, and pretty soon she was the only one he cared about. Sure enough, Xerxes had found himself a new queen. The girl's name was Esther. As far as I'm concerned, he picked the best one. A real beauty. Only thing, though: Esther didn't look Persian to me. She was dark-complexioned but—well, what difference does it make? She made a good-looking queen, and Xerxes was his old self again.

Things went on after that real smooth for about five years. And then one day when Xerxes was holding court, in hopped Haman. Haman was the king's favorite. He had been rising rapidly in our state department over the course of several years. He was actually now number two man in the kingdom. I didn't care for Haman, though; I didn't trust him. I never told Xerxes that—you know, "go with the flow." Anyway, Haman had this little speech all prepared for Xerxes: "Xerxes, scattered throughout your kingdom is a group of people who represent a very disruptive element. These people have their own peculiar laws and they don't pay attention to our Persian ones. It's really to your disadvantage to continue to tolerate them. Now I suggest that we pass a decree that they all be destroyed, and I myself will give personal funds to take care of the matter."

You know what Xerxes said? "Sounds like a good idea, Haman. Follow through on it. And Haman, keep your money. Use government funds." Just like that! He didn't ask Haman who he was talking about. That's just the way Xerxes was sometimes. But it wasn't Xerxes who puzzled me as much as Haman. I couldn't see what Haman was getting at. It wasn't like him to be so solicitous of the king's welfare or so free with his own money unless he was getting something out of it. So I decided to find out what was going on.

The fellow who taught Haman's sons was a friend of mine. You know what it was? Haman wanted to wipe out an entire race of people because of one member of that race. Just because he was irritated by one member, he wanted to destroy them all. Here was his problem: We have in Persia what we call a "citizens' council." This council is composed of representatives from all the national and ethnic groups throughout the kingdom. Every group elects one representative. The purpose of the council is to decide those minor matters that you wouldn't bring to the attention of the king. As number two man in the kingdom, it was Haman's job to drop in on the council occasionally just to check how things were going. Whenever Haman came in, all the representatives from the national groups would bow down to him— except for one, the Jewish representative, who stayed seated in his chair. That's all Haman saw: all the representatives down except for one of them sitting there looking at him.

Okay for you, Mr. Jewish Representative. I'll get you and your people. That's who he was after: the Jews. Haman wanted to liquidate the Jews because their representative wouldn't bow down—and I mean *liquidate* them. I saw a copy of the decree after he got through filling it out. It was brutal. "Destroy, kill, and annihilate all Jews, young and old, women and children, on December 13, and confiscate their property." You couldn't misunderstand it. "Destroy, kill, and annihilate"—that ought to do it—"all Jews, young and old, women and children, on December 13." I thought to myself, *Those poor Jews, they've got eleven months to live.*

As I thought about it, the whole thing didn't make sense to me. As near as I could tell, the reason the Jewish representative wouldn't bow down had something to do with his religious beliefs. But we Persians have always been tolerant of other people's religions. That Haman got my goat. I thought of saying something to Xerxes, but why stick my neck out? Besides that, it was too late anyway. The decree was already being circulated throughout the kingdom.

A few days later I was on the second floor of the palace by an open window when I heard a loud commotion out in the courtyard. I looked out and saw some guy wailing and screaming and making an awful noise. He was a real mess: his hair was tangled, his face smeared with ashes, and his clothes torn. And I thought to myself, *Somebody's got to tell that guy to get away from the palace.* As I was going to the stairway to go down, I bumped into Hatach, the queen's attendant. He seemed to be going the same way I was, only he was carrying some clothes. I asked, "Where are you going?"

"I'm going out to the fellow out there in the courtyard. The queen wants me to take these clean clothes out to him."

"Oh, okay. I'll let you handle it then. And tell him to get away from the palace." I thought to myself, *That Esther. She's all heart. How many queens would care about a bum who needed new clothes?* Hatach came back in, and he still had the clothes with him. "What's the matter? Weren't they his size?"

"Do you know who that is?"

"No, who?"

"It's the Jewish representative."

"Oh. Well he does have something to holler about then"— he'd probably seen the decree—"but why come here around the palace?"

"I don't know. He just gave me this piece of paper and told me to go see Esther about it."

"Here, let me see what it is. Yeah, it's a copy of the decree. But why bother Esther? It's none of her affair."

"I don't know—he just told me to tell her to go and see Xerxes about it."

"See Xerxes about it? Xerxes doesn't know anything about it. He knows about the decree, but he doesn't know it's against the Jews. Besides, why go through the queen? What's she got to do with it?"

"I don't know, but I better do like he said, okay? Let me have it."

"All right."

A little later that day I saw Hatach again. He looked like he was sitting on a powder keg. "Hi, Hatach. How's it going?"

"Harbona? Harbona, you'll never believe it! The queen's a *Jewess!*"

"You're kidding."

"I'm serious."

"No wonder she didn't look Persian to me!"

"Yes, she's Jewish. And when I showed her the decree against all the Jews, she turned real pale but she didn't want to go in and see Xerxes about it. He hasn't called for her for over a month now, you know."

"I know. He's in one of his moods lately."

"Anyway, she told me to go out and talk to the Jewish representative. His name's Mordecai and he's her uncle. She told me to tell him that this was not a good time to go in and see the king. If she went in uninvited, he might do something severe. But Mordecai told me to go back and tell Esther that good time or not, the decree was against all Jews. Being queen won't even save her. And he said, "Maybe she's become queen for such a time as this.""

"So what's Esther going to do?"

"She's going to take her chances and go in and see Xerxes. Harbona, do you think we ought to say something to Xerxes about this?"

"Are you kidding? I'm not about to get caught between Haman, Xerxes, and Esther. Let events take care of themselves." I thought to myself, *Boy oh boy, things are going to get interesting around here! Haman's got a decree out against the Jews because of Mordecai, only he doesn't know that Esther's a Jew and Xerxes is in the dark about everything.*

I didn't have long to wait. A few days later Xerxes was holding court. A side door opened, and Esther appeared. Man, did she look good! She had really fixed herself up. Xerxes took a look—got his scepter down real fast. She came forward, and he could tell by looking at her that something was bothering her. He can be real tender when he wants to be. You should have heard him: "What is it, Esther? What do you want? Name it and you can have it." I thought she would come out with it then, but she didn't. Later I saw it was probably better because Haman wasn't there. Instead she said that that day at noon she had arranged a specially catered lunch, and would Xerxes and Haman join her in the queen's quarters? When lunchtime came, Xerxes again tried to find out what was bothering her, but she wouldn't tell him. Instead she said that she had arranged another lunch for the next day, and would Haman and Xerxes join her again for a second lunch? And I thought, *What is she waiting for? Why doesn't she come out with it?* It's funny that she didn't tell him at that first lunch, because a couple of very interesting things happened before the second lunch. It's strange the way these things fit together. If she had told him at the first lunch, it would have been too soon because of what happened between those two lunches.

The first thing that happened—I got this from the tutor at Haman's house—Haman practically floated home from that first lunch on a cloud. He threw a big party that night for all his friends and told them his personal success story—how much money he had, how he had been promoted rapidly in the state department to the number two spot in the kingdom, and today, the climax, a private luncheon engagement with royalty. The only moth in his Persian rug was Mordecai. Even with the decree out, Mordecai still would not get up and bow down in the council meeting. So that night, Haman and all his friends decided that Mordecai would have to go even before December 13. They made a gallows out of that huge tree in his yard and agreed that first thing in the morning, Haman would talk to Xerxes about hanging the Jewish representative. The second thing that happened between those two lunches—this is really weird—is that night Xerxes had insomnia. He couldn't sleep, though he usually slept like a baby. But about three in the morning I heard it. "Harbona!" I was in the next room.

"Harbona, I can't sleep. Bring something to read to me."

"How about the memoirs of your reign?"

"That'd be fine. Okay."

I got the scrolls and came back and started reading. After I'd been reading for about fifteen minutes, I came to a very interesting paragraph—something about how one day on his way to the council meeting the Jewish representative overheard a plot to assassinate the king, but he had tipped off the queen, foiled the plot, and saved the king's life. Xerxes perked up when I read that. He said, "Yeah, I remember Esther telling me something about that. Harbona, was anything ever done to reward the—what's his name, Mordicky?"

"Mordecai."

"Was anything ever done to reward him?"

I scanned the next few paragraphs. "No."

"Harbona, first thing in the morning you remind me, and we'll take care of that oversight."

"Okay." *This is a fine how-do-you-do. Haman's going to hang him; Xerxes is going to honor him. I can't wait for morning.*

Sure enough, first thing in the morning Xerxes didn't need any reminding. "Are any of my advisers available?"

Somebody says, "Haman's outside."

"Send him in." In came Haman, eager to tell the king his idea about hanging the Jewish representative. Never got the first word out. "Haman, there's a man in my kingdom that I owe a lot to. I'm deeply indebted to this man and I want in some way to show my appreciation publicly so that all will know how much I owe this man. Do you have any ideas, Haman?"

Did Haman have any ideas? He thought it was himself. "Oh yes, Xerxes, yes! Let's see now—yes, whoever it might be, to do right I would put the king's ceremonial robe on him. I would put a gold crown upon his head. I would set him on the king's stallion and then I would have one of your leading officials conduct him through the public streets shouting, 'This is a man the king wants to honor.' "

"Haman, that's good. Look, you're a leading official. You do all of that for the Jewish representative. Mordicky is his name. He'll be getting out of the council meeting about now. Meet him there with all the trimmings you mentioned. And Haman, shout loud, for I owe this man a lot."

Oh, I wish you could have seen Haman's face! One minute he was beaming and then the next he looked whipped. Xerxes turned to me and said, "What's the matter with Haman? Doesn't he feel well?"

"No, I don't think so."

See what I mean about things falling into place? As the morning went by we got glowing reports on Haman's little parade.

When noon came we all went to the queen's quarters for lunch. When Haman got there he looked a little peaked, but he had pretty well pulled himself together. It was a good lunch—Haman, Xerxes, and Esther. While they were lingering over dessert, Xerxes turned to Esther and said, "Esther, something has been bothering you for the past few days. I want you to tell me what it is. Can I do anything for you? Can I give you anything?"

I thought, *Here it comes.* And sure enough—"Yes, Xerxes, there's something you can do for me. There's something you can give me. Give me my life and the life of my people, for we are about to be destroyed, killed, and annihilated."

You should have seen Haman's face. Each one of those words was like a slap. Xerxes says, "What are you talking about Esther? Who would dare do such a thing? Name the man!"

"Haman."

"Haman? Against the—oh, no." And that was too much for Xerxes. He had to go outside onto the patio to think it over.

When Xerxes went out, Haman fell apart. "Esther, I had no idea! I never . . . I would have—Esther, please. Esther, please!" She turned and walked away from him. He got up out of the chair, came over to where she was, got down on his knees, and began to beg, but she wouldn't pay any attention. He began to grab her to make her listen. She had to shove him away. Just then Xerxes came back in, took one look, and came up with the wrong idea.

"Will you molest the queen in my own palace? Cover his face!" And that was it for Haman. When you cover the face, when you drop the death veil, it's all over.

I spoke up then. I don't usually, but it seemed safe. "Uh, Xerxes? Haman had fixed up that huge tree in his yard to hang Mordecai on. Makes a high gallows."

"Hang him on it!" And they did.

They also passed a new decree. You can't take back a former one in Persia but you can pass another one to balance it off. The new decree said that when December 13 came, the Jews could use whatever means they wanted to defend themselves against anyone who came to do them harm. In fact, it even said they could band themselves together and take the initiative against any of their enemies, and the government would ask no questions. You should have seen the Jews dancing in the streets when that one came up!

Later that day I was at that second-floor window, thinking back on the amazing chain of events: Esther being picked queen out of all those girls, Mordecai being the Jewish representative who saved the king's life, Xerxes having insomnia on just the right night. As I looked out the window and saw the Jews celebrating in the streets, looked over the palace wall into the distance and saw Haman dangling from the tree, and thought how all those coincidences had worked together, I thought to myself, *Those Jews—they sure are lucky!*

Now to the God who never slumbers, never sleeps; to the God who knows your coming in and your going out; to the God who hovers around you to preserve you from harm and to give you the future he's planned for you; to our great and good God be glory and praise forever. Amen.

It is human nature to be fascinated with human beings. The first-person monologue, by appealing to that interest, transforms abstract concepts into the stuff of life itself.

The difference between traditional preaching and the first-person narrative resembles the difference between an encyclopedia article about Lindbergh's flight across the Atlantic and a motion picture of the event. The impersonal becomes personal and we experience the adventure for ourselves.

Most biblical narratives, such as those in the chronicles of Samuel and Kings, present the conversations and events of history as stories told in the third person by a narrator-historian. Others, like those in Nehemiah and sections of Acts, sound more personal because they are first-person accounts told by a reporter who was part of the action. In this sermon Don Sunukjian turns the narrative of Esther, recounted in the pages of Scripture in the third person, into a first-person monologue. He presents the account from the vantage point of a bit player who lived as part of the court of Xerxes, king of Persia. By changing the perspective, Sunukjian, without violating the biblical text, presents the story in a fresh, imaginative way.

There are dangers involved in preaching a sermon as narrative. Imagination can degenerate into fantasy and, in an effort to tell a good story, a preacher can scuttle or trivialize the biblical material. Imagination must be linked to the text just as interpretation must be tied to the text. Otherwise the preacher may misrepresent the Scriptures and say in the name of God what God did not say. Sunukjian keeps his imagination in check by his exegesis and historical research, and the central idea of the sermon reflects a dominant theme in Esther.

While some narrative sermons start out telling the story, Sunukjian begins with a formal introduction in which he tells us the foundational concept of Esther and at the same time introduces us to Harbona, the main character of his monologue. With an analogy of a father and a dollhouse, he states his central idea: "You don't see or hear God there, yet he controls everything that happens." Then to orient us to what follows, Sunukjian raises a question that serves as the subject of his narration: "How would this man, who never hears the name of God and yet sees everything that happens, view it?" The full answer to that question waits until the final line of the monologue: *"Those Jews—they sure are lucky!"*

Harbona's monologue follows the chronology of Esther. But, like Esther, it possesses dramatic structure as well. One whimsical formula for constructing a play advises: First, get your hero up a tree. Then put a bear underneath the tree. Finally, get your hero down out of the tree—if you can! This sermon follows that counsel and develops much like a three-act play.

> *Act One:* Background information is presented and the audience is introduced to the central characters. Esther, a Jewess, becomes a Persian queen, and Haman, the villain, schemes to kill his enemy Mordecai by getting Xerxes to wipe out the Jewish people. The heroine is up a tree.
>
> *Act Two:* The heroine leaves the first limb of the tree and scampers up higher among the foliage as the bear tries to get at her. Esther, the queen, tries to foil the villain's plot, but in doing so, she must risk her life.

Act Three: The heroine gets down out of the tree and the Jewish people are delivered. Haman's plan to honor himself honors Mordecai instead, and Haman's gallows erected to execute Mordecai end up hanging him.

The outline of any narrative sermon, therefore, resembles a scenario for a play. Like a playwright, a preacher should develop the action that will transpire in two hundred words or less. As the late Owen Davis once warned a group of aspiring writers: "If your story won't condense into two hundred words, throw it away."

In developing the narrative, Sunukjian does not merely retell the story; he relives it. He employs dialogue to carry on an imagined conversation with other characters and acts out both parts. Dialogue adds variety to a monologue. At another place, he engages in a soliloquy in which he talks to himself. These devices demand that the preacher experience the story and put movements, gestures, and facial expressions into the presentation that paper and ink cannot capture.

The benediction at the end of this narrative does not simply dismiss the audience but provides an effective application of the sermon. It brings the idea of the sermon to a burning focus and deftly shows what difference it should make in life to live within the providence of the sovereign God.

How long does it usually take you to prepare a message?

Between twelve and fifteen hours. I'd always like to have a few more hours. If I had them, I'd probably feel more comfortable about my language or style.

How long did it take you to prepare the message you submitted?

Between thirty-five and forty hours. Esther was an entire book, so I had to get a handle on everything happening in it. In addition, there were unique things to think through. I was developing a minor character and he had to have a personality; I needed to drop hints early in the message about things that would come later; I had to do a lot of reshuffling and memorizing and thinking about how to locate each scene on the platform. Other narrative messages don't take that long.

How long are your sermons normally?

Between thirty and forty minutes.

How do you develop your sermons?

Usually I read the passage in English several times, first of all in the translation that I'm going to preach from and then in other English translations. This gives me a general overview of the passage. It also helps me realize the decisions I'll have to make, not only in translation, but also in exegesis. I try to encounter the passage the way a layperson encounters it when she reads it in English. I jot down whatever questions or observations occur to me or to someone coming to it cold turkey on a Sunday morning.

What next?

Next, I study the text exegetically. If I'm in the New Testament, I open up Arndt-Gingerich and work my way through the Greek text word by word looking up the vocabulary, feeling nuances of each word, noting whatever I can structurally from the grammar, the participles, the imperatives, or the force of the verbs.

When do you consult other resources?

At the end of that process; I usually follow a specific order. First, I look in the exegetical commentaries. They're the most technical works. I'm checking up on my own work, making sure I didn't miss something. Then, I move to the expositional works, such as the *Expositor's Bible Commentaries*.[1] These scholars present a flow of the passage, but are not representing sermons, yet. My final stage is to look at homiletic or sermonic works by others who have preached on this text. I look in my files for articles or messages I have clipped that make this passage relevant to a contemporary audience. I do this last because I want to be faithful to the text, not to some good sermon someone preached. Along the way, I use everything in my library; Bible dictionaries, books on manners and customs, word studies, whatever helps me understand the text and to apply it meaningfully.

I gather you have a filing system?

I have a very extensive file, both an 8½ x 11 and a card file.

How about illustrations? What do you look for in using them?

Very seldom do I use biblical illustrations; even more rarely would I use illustrations from the past. Most of my illustrations come out of contemporary life, and most of those come out of my imagination. I ask myself, "Where does this show up in my life or in the life of my

---

1. Frank E. Gaebelein, ed., *The Expositor's Bible Commentary,* 12 vols. (Grand Rapids: Zondervan, 1976–).

people? What kind of situation would they live through or encounter where this particular biblical truth applies?"

Do you use yourself as an illustration very often?

Yes, but I don't set myself up as a model. I try to look like a human being growing and learning, not somebody who has arrived.

How do you develop the introductions to your sermons?

I try to meet people where they are. I start out with something contemporary; humor, suspense, data, statistics, occupations, something that has a high degree of interest. In the opening paragraph a preacher communicates, "This will be interesting." Then, within the next few paragraphs, I want the audience to say, "This message is one I want to hear." Toward the end of the introduction, I may locate my message very briefly in the context of the passage. I don't spend a lot of time on that. Also toward the end of the introduction, I try to show the listener how to follow the sermon by giving an overview of the broad sections of the sermon. In addition, I give some clue as to whether the sermon will be inductive or deductive. If it's deductive, I will have stated my major idea and probably restated it several times. If the message is inductive, I will have focused on the question that I am asking or the subject I'm discussing.

What then makes an effective introduction?

If I were to identify five ingredients in an effective introduction, they would be: (1) interest in the speaker; (2) interest in the message; (3) some indication of either its deductiveness or its inductiveness; (4) location of the sermon within the biblical context; and (5) some direction on how to listen further.

What was the greatest challenge for you in approaching the biblical text of this sermon?

An attempt to deal with the entire Book of Esther. Not only did I have a massive amount of material to handle in a short period of time, but I had to determine the overall thrust or truth of the book. I determined that the book has to do with God's providential care of his people even when they don't know what he's doing. The next challenge was to get that message across in the same way that the book gets the message across. While the Book of Esther never mentions God, the story had to be told so that the listeners got the point indirectly. A third challenge was picking the major character, someone who could get the story out so that my listeners could get the point without it being stated.

How does a sermon like this develop in your mind?

This character begins to take on a personality. He comes out as a fellow looking out for his own skin. He "goes with the flow." He won't endanger himself. He is a cynic, a pagan. He talks about coincidences. This line gets dropped often to build his perception climaxing in the last line, "Boy, they're sure lucky!" Hopefully, at that point my listener says, "Buddy, you've got it all wrong. That was God putting it all together." Making it happen comes from that; dropping hints in such a way that they seem very natural but they occur at such points that the listener begins to sense God's sovereignty. I also wanted to be historically accurate. Then, after I had the flow of it, I needed to keep all the characters straight before the people. From time to time I reflected six different characters. To do that, I positioned Xerxes always on my stage right, Mordecai out in the audience somewhere stage center left. Then I wrestled with the techniques of representing those different people in separate conversations.

How do you outline a first-person narrative?

I think you would look at it either as a story or a drama in which you have acts and scenes.

Finally, what counsel would you give a young preacher?

The Lord's Word is joyful wisdom. Pass on to your congregation, "Look how good God is and what he has told us. We are fortunate to have access to this kind of wisdom because it makes the difference in how joyful our lives can be."

Chapter 5

Riding the Wind of God
Psalm 127

Duane Litfin

Dr. Duane Litfin is senior pastor of the First Evangelical Church in Memphis, Tennessee. His articles have appeared in *Central States Speech Journal, Western Speech,* and several Christian journals and magazines. He is the author of *Public Speaking: A Handbook for Christians* and co-editor of *Recent Homiletical Thought: A Bibliography.*

It was Socrates who said that the unexamined life is not worth living. Socrates may not have been a Christian, but his was a very Christian notion.

Every Christian should live an examined life. I was reminded of this recently in reading a book on the subject of the Old Testament sabbath. The book raised an interesting question: What is sabbath? Not just the Sabbath Day; what is sabbath rest in general? In other words, what does it mean to take a sabbath?

Sabbath rest does not mean merely a time for recreation, a time when you cease work and start playing. Sabbath is something deeper and more significant than that. It is modeled after the activity of God himself who, having worked six days, took a sabbath. He ceased from his labors, not in order to go off and play, but to examine what he had done. He looked back over those six days and declared, "It's good; that was worth doing."

That is what sabbath rest is and that is what it is for. It is designed to provide us an opportunity to pause and look at what we have done and to decide whether it was worth doing. It is a time to stop and examine our lives.

Unfortunately, for some people an examined life is something to avoid at all costs. There is a great emptiness at the core of their lives, covered only by a veneer of busyness. The busyness is what enables them to avoid looking at the hollow interior. So one must do anything but pause and examine; you must keep on the move, avoid being by yourself, or if you are by yourself, be sure the television is on. Above all, avoid those moments when you pause and examine.

No preacher will ever be able to exhort such people to examine their lives because to examine is to look into an abyss of wasted time, a life that is going nowhere and accomplishing nothing of lasting value.

But there are other people who do not examine their lives for a very different reason. It is not that they need to avoid the truth; rather, they are simply not very good at self-examination. They have not done much of it and they do not know where to begin, or even quite what to look for.

Here is where Psalm 127 may be able to help us. If, like me, you sometimes have a difficult time knowing where to begin examining your life, we have come to the right passage. This brief psalm is perfectly suited to provide the centerpiece, the main criterion of what it is we are to look for when we settle back for a time of self-examination.

As we approach this psalm, we note that it was written by Solomon, and that it is divided into two sections: verses 1–2, and verses 3–5. Verses 1–2 lay out a contrast, while verses 3–5 explore an illustration of that contrast.

The contrast in verses 1–2 is actually unbalanced. Each of this psalm's first seven lines speak about only the first side of the contrast. It is not until we arrive at the last line of verse 2, probably the most important line of the psalm, that we discover the other side of the contrast.

Solomon elaborates the first side of the contrast as follows:

> Unless the LORD builds the house,
>   its builders labor in vain.
> Unless the LORD watches over the city,
>   the watchmen stand guard in vain.

> In vain you rise early
>   and stay up late,
>   toiling for food to eat—(vv. 1–2a)

If you mark your Bibles, you would do well to underline the word *vain*. It occurs three times in these two verses. It is vain; it is empty; it is worthless. This repetition is a pointer to what the psalmist wants to tell us.

It is important for us to sort out what kind of activity Solomon is describing as "vain" in these verses. Contrary to first impressions, he is not referring to activity that is somehow in opposition to God; in other words, he is not saying it is worthless to try to oppose God.

To be sure, this is an important truth and a very biblical one. As a pastor, I often see people attempting to get the best of God, and, of course, it doesn't work. As the old Jim Croche song put it,

SERMON

93

> You don't tug on Superman's cape;
> You don't spit into the wind;
> You don't fool around with a junk yard dog,
> And you don't mess around with Jim.

It's foolish, says this bit of wisdom, to take on something you cannot handle, and that is especially true when that something is God.

But that truth is not really the lesson of this psalm. The psalmist here is talking about a very different kind of activity. He is referring to all of those activities, all of that time, all of those energies one gives to projects that God does not care about, ventures in which he is not interested, or to the success of which he is not committed. You pour your life into that kind of project, says the psalmist, and your efforts will be vain, wasted, down the drain for nothing.

Thus, when we look closely, we discover that the subject of this psalm appears to be spending; not so much the spending of our money, but the spending of our very lives.

There are three things we typically spend: our money, our time, and our energy. Yet money should not be categorized with time and energy. It is as if we were to speak of hydrogen, oxygen, and ice. Hydrogen and oxygen combine to make water, but ice is one of the forms that water takes. You do not categorize those three things together. So it is with time, energy, and money. Money is simply one of the forms that our time and energy take.

There are people who seem to have unlimited quantities of money. But no one has unlimited quantities of time and energy. Every one of us has a restricted amount of both. That's why as commodities they are far more basic and important than money. So let us not concern ourselves for the moment with the spending of money; let us allow this psalm to focus our attention on the budgeting of our time and energy. If we set that in order, how we spend our money will take care of itself.

Psalm 127 is about how we spend our limited quantities of time and energy, the most precious commodities that we possess. And spend them we inevitably do.

We recently enjoyed a visit from my parents, so that there were three generations in the home. First there were the children who seem to have boundless energy; they just go on and on. Their whole life seems to lie in front of them and they have little sense of their limitations, either of time or energy. They think they can do anything. Their bodies can take anything. Well, I'm forty-three now and I know better. Even at age forty-three, which for many still sounds young, I can begin to feel my limitations. In fact, that is one of the characteristics of the so-called mid-life syndrome: You begin measuring your life from the end rather than the beginning; you start asking the question, How much time do I have left? Then there were my parents, in their sixties, who feel this process even more keenly. And then you visit the nursing homes, or you visit a terminally ill patient in the hospital and you are looking at people whose reserves of time and energy are almost spent—there is not much left. You become profoundly aware of how limited are the quantities of these two basic commodities the Lord has given us, our time and energy.

The psalmist's question is, How do we spend them? What do

we spend them for? That's what this psalm is about, spending our lives. And what he is saying is that if we are spending our days on projects in which the Lord has no interest, the success of which he does not care about at all, we are wasting our time. We will look back and say, "I wasted my life. It accomplished nothing of any lasting significance."

Notice that the issue is not whether we build the house; the house may well be built, but in the end the question will be, so what? The business may well be established, but if Christ was not in it, what of any lasting value was accomplished? The practice may well thrive, but in the long run, if this is anything other than what God wants me to do, what difference can it make? Unless the Lord is interested in accomplishing this particular task and it's one of his projects, then every ounce of energy we pour into it, every moment we give to it, every effort we spend to build it is wasted, meaningless, worthless.

This, then, is the one side of the psalmist's contrast. But there is also the other side, which we discover in the final line of verse 2: "For He gives to His beloved even in his sleep."

To appreciate fully this line, we must remember that this is poetry, and poetry is not always easy to read. We have to give ourselves to poetry and explore it. Poetry is compact and full of images; so in order to understand it, we must go slowly and unpackage the author's meaning.

We have in this tightly packed line several poetic allusions. Do you recall what a poetic allusion is? It's the sort of reference which, if you do not understand its background, you will miss the poet's point. For example, in a book of poetry on the subject of Oxfordshire in England, I recently ran across a poem by the poet laureate of Britain, John Betjeman, entitled, *Summoned by Bells.* In this poem we find these lines:

> Take me my Centaur Bike down Linton Road
> Gliding by newly planted almond trees
> Where the young dons with wives in tussore clad
> Were building in the morning of their lives
> Houses for future dragons . . .

SERMON

95

There are a number of easily understood references here: Linton Road, the Centaur Bike, the dons who are the tutors at Oxford University—but "building houses for future dragons"? What could that possibly mean?

This poem is about the neighborhood in Oxford where we lived for two years. We lived just off Linton Road, as had John Betjeman many years before. In fact, Betjeman also attended the Dragon School, the elite private boys' school in that neighborhood past which I rode my bicycle every day to travel to the library. Hence Betjeman's poetic allusion to "dragons." This is one of the beauties of poetry; there is so much folded into it that it merits our study and concentration.

Modern poets do this to us all the time—but so did the ancient Hebrew poets, and we are unlikely to find a more tightly compressed line in the psalter than this. Let's look at several of the poetic allusions in that single line.

The word translated "beloved" here is the Hebrew word *yadid.* Do you remember the name that God gave to Solomon when he was born? In 2 Samuel 12:24–25 we read:

> Then David comforted his wife Bathsheba, and he went to her and lay with her. She gave birth to a son, and they named him Solomon. The LORD loved him; and because the LORD loved him, he sent word through Nathan the prophet to name him *Jedidiah.*

Solomon was named by the Lord himself: Jedidiah, the *yadid* of *Yahweh,* "Beloved of the Lord." Built into the Lord's own name for Solomon is this word *yadid,* "beloved."

How utterly fitting. When you think of Solomon, what comes to your mind? His wisdom, of course. Listen to 1 Kings 3:5: "At Gibeon the LORD appeared to Solomon during the night in a dream, and God said, 'Ask for whatever you want me to give you.'" As we know, Solomon asked for wisdom and the Lord approved; he gave Solomon the special gift of his wisdom. "Then Solomon awoke—and he realized it had been a dream." God's greatest gift to his beloved Solomon was given to him while he was sleeping.

The poetic allusion to the "beloved" in Psalm 127 is, then, first and foremost to Solomon, but it serves as an example of how God gives to all his "chosen people, holy and dearly loved" (Col. 3:12). Not only does the beloved one receive the fruit of his labor; he also receives dividends even when he is resting.

This reference to God's beloved one, then, reaches far beyond Solomon. In fact, it makes for an interesting study to pursue the concept of the "beloved of the Lord" throughout the Bible. Perhaps the most striking passage of all is Deuteronomy 33:12, where, speaking of the tribe of Benjamin, Moses says,

> Let the beloved (*yadid*) of the LORD rest secure in him,
> for he shields him all day long,
> and the one the LORD loves rests between his shoulders.

The beloved one is the one who dwells between the shoulders of God. Do you recognize the image? The beloved of God "rides piggyback" on the Lord.

It is as if a son were to join his father on a long journey. As they travel together, the boy becomes weary and cannot continue. So the father takes his son onto his back and carries him. He carries him piggyback, so that even while the son sleeps, he still makes progress. Why? Because he is traveling on his father's journey.

The beloved of the Lord dwells between the shoulders of his heavenly Father. That's essentially what the psalmist has in mind when he says, "for He gives to His beloved even in his sleep." The contrast here is not between the one who works hard and the one who sits back and does nothing; this is no commendation of slothfulness. It is a poetic contrast between the one who works very hard, spending long toilsome hours for a meaningless project, and so winds up with nothing to show for his efforts; as against the one who invests himself in a project the Lord is doing and finds himself earning dividends beyond expectation.

Let's see if we can capture this contrast visually by conjuring up two very different pictures. The first has to do with a fellow named Sisyphus. Do you remember Sisyphus? Probably not, but perhaps you have heard the term *a Sisyphean task*—an endless, difficult, and pointless task.

If you look up Sisyphus in your dictionary, you will discover that he was a mythological figure in Homer's *Odyssey,* a Greek poem written almost a millennium before Christ. Poor Sisyphus. Homer portrays him in hell, and this was his punishment:

> And I saw Sisyphus in violent torment, seeking to raise a monstrous stone with both of his hands. Verily he would brace himself with hands and feet, and thrust the stone toward the crest of a hill, but as often as he was about to heave it over the top, the weight would turn it back, and then down again to the plain would come rolling the ruthless stone. But he would strain again and thrust it back, and the sweat flowed down from his limbs, and dust rose up from his head.[1]

Poor Sisyphus, doomed to an eternity of rolling that huge stone up the hill, only to have it roll back down; only to struggle with it back up the hill, only to have it roll back down; over and over throughout eternity. Long hours, difficult labor, in a pointless and meaningless task.

Homer intended Sisyphus to be a sad figure. But sadder still is the thought that many people today spend their days on equally worthless pursuits. Struggling week in and week out, rising up early and sitting down late, eating the bread of painful toil, all in order to accomplish eternally meaningless projects, projects about which Christ could not care less and which will have no lasting value. They are our projects, not his; we may be committed to their success, but the Lord is not. All of that energy, all of that effort and precious time wasted, being poured down the drain for something that has no future.

But now contrast that strange image of Sisyphus with an entirely different picture. We stepped out of our home recently only to discover rising across our neighborhood and passing unbelievably fast, no more than two or three hundred feet up in the sky, a beautiful, vividly colored hot air balloon. It was a

---

1. Homer, *Odyssey* (ed. A. T. Murray; trans. T. E. Page) 11.593–600.

huge thing with three people in the gondola hanging beneath the billowing colors. They were just high enough that you could still have called out to them. They were so close you could see the people easily, but they were moving amazingly fast across the sky.

Have you ever ridden in a hot air balloon? They say it's a lot like sailing with the wind. You may be moving very quickly, but there is complete silence and no sense of any wind. How can that be? The answer is simple. You may be traveling forty miles per hour, but you are riding on the wind, so to speak; it's carrying you with it. And so, as you travel *with* the wind, there is no sense of your own motion except as you see the earth glide by beneath you. The journey is startlingly quiet and peaceful.

That's the kind of thing Solomon has in mind on the positive side of the contrast: the one who lives with the wind of God at his back.

The beloved of the Lord rides piggyback on God when he pours his time and effort into projects to which God is committed; they are his heavenly Father's projects and the child is simply along for the ride. To such a one the Lord promises eternal fruit for his labor. There may well be hard work, but it will be to great purpose and of genuine value. And not only that, all of the hard work becomes capital that earns dividends even while we are not working. Why? Because like a father carrying his son on his back, even while we are asleep, God is still at work, moving ahead to accomplish his purposes. Thus it is that the one who invests his time and effort in Christ's projects appears to move through life "with the wind of God at his back."

As a pastor I see both kinds of people so very clearly. On the one hand, I see people who are struggling with life. All of their existence seems in the end to be wearisome because they are committed to projects and goals in which Jesus Christ is not in the least interested. They are their own projects and goals, not the Lord's.

But I also see other people who seem to ride the wind of God. As these Christians move through life, they see great purpose and meaning in their work, and such fruit and blessing that they look up and say, "Where did that come from?" The difference is that they are giving themselves to the projects of the Lord; they have set his goals before them. They are riding piggyback on the Lord.

Obviously, then, the key, as we attempt to examine our lives, is to ask, What are the tasks to which I am giving my time and my energy? The mainspring of my life is winding down. I can see it and feel it. What are my goals? What are the projects to which I am committed? Are they Christ's projects, assigned to me, or have I created them for myself?

To help with this kind of self-examination, Solomon offers us a concrete example of the kind of project that is worthy of our lives. "Look," he says, "here is a case in point."

> Sons are a heritage from the LORD,
> children a reward from him.

Solomon might have chosen any of several illustrations, but children are perhaps the best example because they leave so little room for ambiguity. Children are precisely the sort of project that this psalm has been commending from the outset. They are not merely our projects; they are God's projects assigned to us.

Notice the subtle and intricate poetic connection between how we conceive children, and Solomon's reference to God giving to His beloved even in his sleep. Children are the product of that portion of our lives that we spend in repose, yet they are the most beneficial blessings we possess. The poetic beauty of this psalm should not be missed.

Solomon is operating on the sound biblical assumption that if we have children, we may be assured that they have been assigned to us specifically by the Lord. The purpose of a public ceremony of baby dedication is expressly to acknowledge this fact. Contrary to what people may sometimes think or feel, we do not have children by mistake or accident. Solomon reminds us that our children are a project custom-tailored by the Lord specifically for us. And as such, they are a venture into which we can confidently invest our time and effort with eternal dividends.

According to Solomon, the attention we give to our children will continue to pay rewards all the days of our lives. That's what he means when he says:

> Like arrows in the hand of a warrior.
> are sons born in one's youth.
> Blessed is the man whose quiver is full of them.
> They will not be put to shame
> when they contend with their enemies in the gate.

Children are one of the best investments of our time and energy, both for this life and for eternity. They are, as Solomon says, the parents' projectiles. Like arrows in the hand of a warrior, so are children in the hand of their parents. They are the means by which parents reach out and make their greatest impact on time and eternity. For good or for ill, we multiply our influence through our children.

I was thinking this week of my own ministry. Here I am pastoring a congregation in a city which my parents had never before visited. Yet what this congregation is seeing in me is to a large extent the product of what my father and mother invested in me all those years in our home at 804 Symes, Royal Oak, Michigan. They are, in a very real sense, ministering in this community today, through me. And they assure me that what they see me doing here remains as one of God's greatest delights to them in their own lives. Thus do they continue to receive dividends on time and effort they invested in me years ago.

I saw a father send his son to the mission field this past week. From that home a projectile is going out to touch France for Christ. Another of their children, a daughter, is a missionary to Pakistan. Another is a godly housewife here in the States. All of the time and energy those parents poured into those three children was invested for time and for eternity. Nothing else those parents did with their time could have been more important than what they invested in their children.

Those who dedicate their children to the Lord, says Solomon, will not be ashamed. Such children will be the crown of a full

SERMON

101

life. In our old age, when the accuser of the brethren stands to challenge us in the gate, charging us with a wasted life, godly children will constitute his prime refutation. They are the best example of a divine project which has ongoing rewards.

But they are not the only example. Not all of our time can be invested in our children, and not everyone will have children. Children are a prime example of a divinely worthwhile project, but there are many others.

For example, if you are a business or professional person, think of how you are spending your life. If you are spending your time and energy to build a company or a position or a practice, in order to become affluent, to grow in influence and prestige and personal comfort, there is nothing that I know of to suggest that Jesus Christ is the least bit interested in your success. You're on your own. You are involved in a project of your own choosing, not his.

On the other hand, if you are committed to the business or professional world in order to use the gifts God has given you to build Christ's kingdom, then you have enlisted in one of God's choicest projects. Your time and energy are being invested with eternal dividends. Your efforts will be directed toward functioning as a beachhead for righteousness, and for the gospel of Jesus Christ, wherever God has put you. Like Daniel shining in a pagan world, personal profit will have become unimportant; the glory of God, manifested in all you do and say and demonstrated in the sheer excellence and integrity of your work and witness, becomes your priority.

Or let us suppose you are working to provide yourself with a home. To the extent that you are giving of your life's energies to build a place of personal luxury, beautifully furnished, in the right neighborhood, designed to indulge your personal tastes and, not incidently, to impress those who may be watching, God's Word would seem to indicate that your efforts are being eternally wasted. You are pouring your most precious possessions—your time and your energy—down the drain of self-indulgence.

On the other hand, if you make decisions about what sort of house you need in the light of God's purposes for a home, everything you invest there may be of eternal value. For instance, viewing your home as the prime place to model godly values to your children will mean that the choices you make will be geared to God's purposes; treating the house as a center of Christian hospitality and as a launching pad for the gospel in your neighborhood will dictate God-centered decisions. In this way the efforts you put into providing a genuinely Christian home wind up invested for eternity.

It was C. S. Lewis, I believe, who said, "Everything that is not eternal, is eternally out of date." As usual with Lewis, it is a well-turned phrase. But Solomon expressed the thought with still greater charm long before Lewis, in Psalm 127.

Are you willing to pause and examine your life, to evaluate those tasks into which you are pouring your time and energy? Are they your projects or Christ's? Do you ride between the shoulders of your heavenly Father, or are you traveling your own road? Solomon says the value of our life's work is only as good as the cause for which it is expended. If we choose wisely, we can invest our time and energy for eternity by spending them for Jesus Christ. It's a thought that ought to guide all of our self-examination.

SERMON

103

Simply flip through the pages of the Old Testament and glance at the layout on the page of any modern translation and you'll discover God is a poet. Poetry turns up everywhere. In fact, poetry makes up about one-third of the entire Bible and takes up as much space as the entire New Testament.[2] Biblical Hebrew had no word for "poetry." The short terse lines of a psalm or proverb, however, along with their metaphors and similes, set poetic literature apart from the prose found in a book like Leviticus.[3] A preacher true to the Scriptures, therefore, must understand Hebrew poetry, how a poet communicates his message, and how a preacher communicates that poetic message through a sermon.

Duane Litfin explains the imagery of Psalm 127, but he does not subject his congregation to a dry lecture on Hebrew poetry. As a preacher, Litfin tackles a larger question, "How should

2. Tremper Longman III, *Literary Approaches to Biblical Interpretation* (Grand Rapids: Zondervan, 1987), p. 119.

3. For a discussion of biblical poetry, see James L. Kugel, *The Idea of Biblical Poetry* (New Haven: Yale University Press, 1981); Robert Alter, *The Art of Biblical Poetry* (New York: Basic Books, 1985); and Longman, *Literary Approaches.*

we invest our time and energy for what counts in life?" and turns to the psalmist for an answer. To get to the solution given in the psalm, however, the preacher must become a teacher. Able expositors respond to a congregation's questions and increase a congregation's knowledge. In this sermon, Litfin devotes a significant amount of time to a discussion of poetry in general and the specific images within the psalm. In handling these poetic elements in the passage, he draws parallels to a pop song in the twentieth century and more directly with the poem *Summoned by Bells* by John Betjeman. He demonstrates that explanation in a sermon does not have to sound as dull or complicated as instructions on how to assemble a Christmas toy. Just as important, Litfin does not talk down to his congregation, but introduces his excursion by saying, "We have to give ourselves to poetry and explore it." As an effective teacher, a preacher helps his hearers learn without insulting them or talking down to them.

A well-crafted sermon has two centers, one in the Bible and the other in the congregation. A skillful expositor exegetes both. While Litfin works in the psalm, he works with his audience as well. He remembers that without the Bible he has nothing to say, but without his congregation, a sermon has no place to go. Litfin does not give everything away in his introduction, but keeps a sense of tension alive until his second major point, also a full, strong statement of the central idea of the sermon. The development of the sermon in outline form looks like this:

    I. The value of our life's work is only as good as the cause for which it is expended.
       A. The issue in Psalm 127 is how we spend our lives.
       B. Everything we spend on projects in which God is not interested is wasted.
       C. Everything we spend on God's projects is invested.
    II. We can invest our lives for eternity by spending them on God's projects.

A. Children are the psalmist's prime example of a divinely ordained project.

B. There are other numerous examples of God's projects as well.

The sermon takes the shape of a principle applied. It moves by induction up to the second major point, where a fundamental principle is stated. After that, the sermon applies the principle to rearing children but then moves beyond the psalm to suggest other spheres in which this principle can work out in experience. This particular form focuses strongly on application and always has a ring of relevance to it.

Litfin states his big idea several times throughout the sermon and then uses a quote from C. S. Lewis to state it again in the conclusion. In developing his points, he constantly moves from an abstract statement to a concrete, specific example that nails the sermon into life. He employs a number of illustrations from a variety of sources: Greek classics, pop music, science, poetry, hot air balloons, and his own experiences.

COMMENTARY

107

It is important to notice the preacher's stance. He does not talk to the audience about the Bible, although the passage is clearly explained, but instead talks to his hearers about them and their decisions from the Bible. That is the stance of effective biblical preaching. It is not a lecture or an essay, but a conversation with a congregation.

How long does it usually take you to prepare a message?

Probably in the neighborhood of ten to fifteen hours.

How long did it take you to prepare the message you submitted?

This particular message was closer to fifteen hours because of the exegetical puzzles and the enigmatic references that must be understood.

How long are your sermons normally?

My sermons average somewhere between thirty and forty minutes.

How do you develop the biblical content of your sermons?

It varies with the message and with the passage. I do whatever it takes to exegete the passage. Sometimes it takes a great deal; other times it is there on the surface waiting for me as I open the text. I'm not going to invest hours in exegeting something I already understand.

You use helps, then?

Yes, I'm shameless. I use anything that is useful, both in exegesis and in homiletics. I'm a great believer in commentaries. I think it's best to bring in the commentaries later in the process than earlier. I depend on anything that will prompt me, stimulate me, give me insights or little glimmers. Commentaries don't answer questions as much as they stimulate me. I use the original languages (my Greek is stronger than my Hebrew today). I don't translate a passage from scratch. That's a waste of time given the helps and resources that we have.

Where do you get your illustrations?

I'm a great believer in the illustration file, but I don't always follow through on it the way I'd like to. It requires an enormous discipline to keep the file fresh so that it's usable and useful in your preaching ministry. I find that my file lets me down because I've let the file down.

Where do you get most of your supporting material, then?

The bulk of it comes from the tools that are at hand—what I have in my mind, my heart, my memory, my recent experiences, my imagination, sources, something in the commentary that triggers something in me. I will take them from any place I can get them.

You've taught homiletics at Dallas Seminary, and now you're a pastor. What changes has that brought in your ministry?

A pastoral ministry drains your creative energies. When you spend three and four hours with people whose lives are falling apart and you try to help them and then you try to work on a sermon . . . the well is dry. Apparently, I only have so much creative energy. Eleven o'clock Sunday morning is always staring at you, and you have only x number of hours. When you are in seminary (in my case, as a professor), you are preparing far fewer messages and you have time to give to preparation because your schedule is much more your own. In the pastorate, so much of your time is not your own. It is dictated by things over which you have little or no control.

What are you saying, then, about preaching in your role as a pastor?

The impact of coming back to the pastorate, therefore, has hit me in the sheer amount of speaking I have to do. Proverbs says that in many words transgression is unavoidable, and I feel that. Not only that, but all of this speaking gobbles up huge amounts of material. It eats up material like television. When you're a seminary professor, you have lots of stimulation, and the outflow is much more restricted. That reverses when you go into the pastorate. The outflow is heavy duty, but the time you have to replenish becomes more limited as the church gets bigger. I feel that in my lack of supporting material, my lack of time to polish and the need to take shortcuts. I have to settle for more limited objectives.

How do you develop the introductions to your sermons?

You can either introduce the sermon as a whole or you can introduce your first point. Almost always, I introduce the entire message. I look for a basic pattern in developing a sermon. I introduce the idea of the entire message in the introduction and then return to it. I want to have echoes of where I started, so people have a feeling of coming full circle, the sense when I'm through, "We've covered this ground; we're home; we're where he said we would go." I try to see the sermon itself as an answer to a question. Therefore, I have to ask, "What's the question to which, if somebody asked it, I would offer this kind of material as a response?" I try to focus that to get clearly in mind what I'm answering, why people need to hear this. I raise that need in the introduction. You can't do this until your sermon is in hand. So, at least for me, introductions get done last.

What was the greatest challenge for you in approaching the biblical text of this sermon?

The challenge was to preach a poem without destroying it. Preaching a psalm can be like taking a flower apart. By the time you're finished, you've got a bunch of petals lying on the table but you don't have a flower anymore. I tried to make this almost an excursion into literary criticism. I wanted people to come away understanding this psalm better because I had explored it.

Another difficulty lay in the exegetical problems to be solved in Psalm 127. The trickiest was in the line about God giving to His beloved even in His sleep. How do we translate that? Depending on how you translate it, you take off in two different directions. If God is "giving sleep" to His beloved, rather than "in His sleep," you start on a different flow of thought. Even when you've made that decision in translation, you still struggle with an enigmatic phrase having poetical allusions.

Why did you take your sermon in the direction you did?

I was trying to give a glimpse of how poetry works. Most people today do not read poetry. So, I surfaced an example of poetic allusion. Unless you do this, the explanation of "the beloved" sounds farfetched. The author packages poetic allusions into the text, and we have to unpack them to get the most out of the poetry. Only in this way can an audience understand what Solomon is doing in his poem. That has further implications as to whether or not they will hear what God is saying to them in this psalm. The sermon fell naturally into two major sections, because the psalm has two very distinct movements.

Is your sermon inductive or deductive?

Both. The first point is designed to surface the principle of the psalm. Then out of that principle, you're saying, "Look. Here are some cases in point." So, I moved from the principle to specific application. It's a move from the details of the text to its overall principle back down to the details of life. In other words, this is a "principle-applied" sermon.

What skills have stayed with you out of your early training in homiletics?

More than skills, I came away with deep commitments. A commitment to the Word, a commitment not to bore people, a commitment to be clear. As a means of being clear, I focus what I'm doing on a single unit of discourse. That, in turn, allows me to have this so-called "big idea."

Chapter 6

He Who Has Ears to Hear . . .
Jeremiah 1

Bo Matthews

Bo Matthews serves as pastor of Hinson Memorial Baptist Church in Portland, Oregon. Previously, he served as pastor of congregations in Delaware and New York.

Centuries before Jeremiah preached to the kings of Judah, men communicated in emergencies by fire. Fortified cities, housing crack army units and built to withstand prolonged assault and siege, also served as centers of communication.

Fire signals in the night proclaimed the advance of an alien army, counterattack, defeat, or "all is well." Men at designated signal stations saw the fires and passed on the message to the next fortified city, which in turn communicated to another.

The system still worked in Jeremiah's day. Fortified cities dotted the Judean countryside. The greatest of them, the one for whose sake the others were, was Jerusalem.

On spring and summer nights in the year 589 B.C. signal fires burned with an urgency of life and death. And one by one those fires went out. The Babylonian hordes extinguished them forever.

The Chaldeans came to Jerusalem, and Jerusalem held fast. But of all the other fortified cities only Lachish and Azekah did the same. From the ruins of Lachish archaeologists have retrieved a handful of letters that arrived in the city during the very days of the Babylonian siege. One of the letters appears to have come from Jerusalem, and its eyewitness simplicity is heartbreaking:

"We are looking for the signal stations of Lachish, according to all the signals you are giving, because we cannot see the signals of Azekah."

Azekah had fallen. Within months Lachish fell. In July 587, Jerusalem's food supply ran out, and on that very day the Babylonians breached the city wall.

Before they left, they had destroyed the temple, torn down the city wall, massacred or deported nearly the whole population, and burned everything in sight.

In a sense the Old Testament serves no other purpose than to explain Jerusalem's catastrophe. Of those precious thirty-nine documents none stands so near that sadness than the Word of the Lord that came to Jeremiah. We label him "the Weeping Prophet," but we should weep, too, if Washington or Los Angeles lay smoldering in ruins.

No other Old Testament figure, except David, comes through to the modern reader in such human terms. Jeremiah tells how it felt to live through the holocaust. Jeremiah survived the holocaust. Best of all, he unfolds the meaning of the holocaust.

And that secured his writings their place in the sacred text of Israel and the church. For what a people in catastrophe want is meaning. Time and time again the prophet asks the urgent question: Why has God done this to us? He answers in oracle after oracle distended with meaning.

I just described Jeremiah's writings as "the Word of the Lord that came to Jeremiah." On every page we read, Thus saith the Lord, the Word of the Lord came to me, the Lord declares.

In the bluntest way the prophet claimed to be God's mouthpiece. But Jeremiah was not alone in this. Many of his peers were prophets. They too claimed to be God's mouthpiece, and their message contradicted Jeremiah's. Jeremiah's message presented in fact a dissenting, minority view.

But when Nebuchadnezzar had finished with Jerusalem, some of the survivors came upon the writings of Jeremiah, which in some jumbled fashion had been preserved. They read them. They remembered the Babylonian armies. They remembered Jerusalem in shambles.

They drew the only logical conclusion: however much despised, Jeremiah had spoken the truth. It was he, not the muttering majority, who had spoken the thoughts of God to Israel. When Jeremiah spoke, God had been speaking. But who in those days had been listening?

Where did Jeremiah get his start? What convictions, what experiences sent him forth into public life? Can the Word of God be renewed in our day? On these matters it is best to begin by allowing the prophet to speak for himself. That awaits us in the opening chapter of the Book of Jeremiah.

The opening verses of Jeremiah have breath and blood in them. They suggest urban sounds and smells. They conjure up the picture of politicians wheeling and dealing in smoke-filled rooms. You can hear the tramp of armies and the screams of their victims.

And in the middle of it all, the Word of the Lord came to Jeremiah. It is inviting to paraphrase verse 2: "The Word of the Lord came to Jeremiah as life in Judah reached a fever pitch."

SERMON

117

Three kings come to the fore here. Josiah tried to do in the religious life of Judah what Ronald Reagan tried to do in the economic life of America: undo the sins of his predecessors. You can, if many things work right, legislate economic change; the very effort to legislate religious reform is doomed to fail, and Josiah failed.

His son, Jehoiakim, a vain and lavish man, undid the religious efforts of his father, had nothing but contempt for Jeremiah, and, like other bad men before and since, died just before the nation he governed paid dearly for his disastrous policies. The Babylonians invaded Judah and Jerusalem for the first time.

His successor, the irresolute Zedekiah, ruled over Judah during the second Babylonian invasion which destroyed the temple and the city of Jerusalem.

And Jeremiah saw it all, lived through it all, preached through it all. When Jeremiah spoke to the human situation of his day, God was speaking. But who in those days was listening?

Now, what does it mean to say, "God was speaking", or "God is speaking"? It means, first of all, that human circumstances have a divine meaning. Josiah's attempt at reform was more than a king's decree. Jehoiakim's folly was more than political action. The Babylonian destruction of Jerusalem was more than just an act of war. They were the human means by which God's purpose was being carried out. God was speaking.

But we could never know what God was saying merely by living through those circumstances. The destruction of Jerusalem seemed to contradict all the purposes of God. If human events are the language God speaks, we need an interpreter. Jeremiah was such a man. How did he become such a man that he should step into the ring of fire and speak the thoughts of God to the sons of Adam? Verses 4–10 tell us much.

"The word of the LORD came to me, saying, 'Before I formed you in the womb I knew you, before you were born I set you apart; I appointed you as a prophet to the nations.' "

We often hear people say, "God called me to do such and such." And we often ask, "What does it mean to be called by God?" It is not the whole answer, but it is a necessary part of the answer to say that being called by God involves a feeling and a fear that God wants you to do a task for him that very few can do.

Not that you are better than others, or worthy to do the task, or especially qualified to do it, or even want to do it; but that God wants you to do it and will make up for your deficiencies.

And if God wants you to do it, there has never been a time he did not want it. The journey in your mother's womb, the nurturing from birth to adulthood served to bring you to the day when his eternal intentions entered your conscious life, wakened new emotions, and called you to take the path chosen for you.

Being called by God also involves a fear. The fear as well as the feeling seems necessary to the experience of being called by God. So many great men have shrunk from the prospects of being God's chosen servant for a chosen task.

It was Moses who, on hearing God's chosen path for him, asked "Who am I, that I should go to Pharaoh and bring the Israelites out of Egypt?"

When time came to present Saul to the tribes of Israel as their first king, he could not be found; he had hidden himself among the baggage.

Those who know will tell you: fear at being called by God is not polite humility; it is reality striking just the right note on the keyboard of our feelings.

Jeremiah's initial response is: "Ah, Sovereign LORD, I do not know how to speak; I am only a child." It is Jeremiah's only protest.

The Lord waives it aside with the further command, "You must go to everyone I send you to, and say whatever I command you." He promises (v. 8) to protect Jeremiah from the dangers that lay ahead. "Then the LORD reached out his hand and touched my mouth and said to me, 'Now I have put my words in your mouth.' "

What words? What meteor from the heavens now rested upon Judean hillsides? What intentions of the mind of God were now implanted in the mind of man?

SERMON

119

"See, today I appoint you over nations and kingdoms to uproot and tear down, to destroy and overthrow, to build and to plant."

In the din of heart rebellion and fatal foreign policy the rooting up and tearing down take precedence in Jeremiah's ministry. The themes of planting and building provide a subtle counterpoint to the warnings of disaster. We must hear both point and counterpoint or else we miss the Word of God.

And so the interpreter is ready. The tongue of God on earth is loosed. But how shall we know it is the tongue of God that speaks? So many speak, so many at cross-purposes, so many in loud and angry voices or soft, alluring voices.

What are the marks of the Voice of God? Two visions and a promise answer this question which was perhaps also Jeremiah's question. The first vision occupies verses 11–12.

"The word of the LORD came to me: 'What do you see, Jeremiah?' 'I see the branch of an almond tree,' I replied. The LORD said to me, 'You have seen correctly, for I am watching to see that my word is fulfilled.' "

The assurance given to Jeremiah and to us, his distant heirs— the first mark of God's authentic Word to man—is its reliability.

God utters forth his Word and watches for the day of its ripening in human life.

When we forget it, he remembers. When circumstances contrive to cancel out his Word, he remembers. When we despair, he prepares to carry out his word. The Scriptures bear witness to the vigilance of God in keeping watch to see that his intentions are fulfilled.

That is why we cherish these words of days long past; in them we learn the authentic Word of God for present days and present trouble—authentic and therefore reliable.

A second vision gives another mark of that authentic Word. Verses 13–16 say, "The word of the LORD came to me again: 'What do you see?' 'I see a boiling pot, tilting away from the north,' I answered."

The Lord interprets that vision as an image of invading armies from the north who will come against Jerusalem as instruments of wrath. To preach this coming wrath of God will be the heavy burden Jeremiah bears.

The reason given for his coming wrath marks the message as God's authentic Word. "I will pronounce my judgments on my people because of their wickedness in forsaking me" (v. 16). Whatever else the Lord may say, when he truly speaks to us through his chosen servants, he speaks concerning idolatry, our exchange of the truth of God for a lie.

The doctor seldom enjoys telling his patient the worst. All of us shrink from bearing ill tidings. The servant of God had rather not expose the follies of the human heart.

But what does it avail to speak of beauty, strength, and brains when the X ray shows a large mass on the lung? That one spot endangers all the rest unless removed.

All sin is a turning away from God, a suppression of the truth about God. Unless checked and removed, it will bring down on us a ruin of immense proportion.

God's authentic Word will always address us at our point of greatest need—our sin. Those who claim to be his servants and speak his Word but never expose sin against God, we may safely ignore. They have no word from God.

But you can understand why his true servants often quail before their task. No one looks for such a task; it is laid on him, and its weight is great.

Consider Jeremiah again. "Get yourself ready! Stand up and say to them whatever I command you. Do not be terrified by them, or I will terrify you before them."

God promises Jeremiah unusual protection. But the terror and the danger are real. As verse 19 says, "they will fight against you." An authentic Word from God is marked by opposition. Those who preach merely their own mutterings will be ignored. He who conveys the mind of God to sinners will be opposed.

And so in a little town within the territorial boundaries of Benjamin, a three-mile walk from the gates of Jerusalem, the Flame of Love descends.

The young son of a Jewish priest took his place in the Council of the Lord. To him was given the Word of God for the remnant of Israel and the kings of Judah.

SERMON

121

As events would prove, his message of sin and judgment to come was reliable and did not merit the hatred and suspicion that befell him. When Jeremiah spoke, God was speaking. But who in his day was listening?

Not many, to hear the Old Testament tell it. Jeremiah reports that resistance to the Word of God was so virile as to survive the destruction of Jerusalem, and to survive among the leftovers of Jewish society who had gone into self-imposed exile in Egypt.

Jeremiah himself may have died in Egypt. We could hardly say he died a success. As measured by his own hopes for Judah and by the intent of his preaching, he died a conspicuous failure.

Under the weight of that failure we may ask if it matters that God speaks to our human circumstances. In one obvious way it matters very much, as the ruins of Jerusalem testify. The Word of God through Jeremiah had often warned of that possibility.

But of the other option—a repentant Jerusalem, her political integrity preserved among the imperial kingdoms of the earth, her worship untainted by the ancient world's encircling idolatry—of that option what shall we say?

Its proclamation in Jeremiah's day came to nothing but words. To the political realists of his day the words of repentance seemed unpromising as a method of preventing national disaster.

But Jeremiah spoke the mind of God. The seeming irrelevance of his words to an actual military and political danger must not blind us; if Jeremiah spoke the mind of God, then he spoke the truth. Man must hear the truth, must be given a chance to believe it, and alter his life accordingly.

It is better for the sun to shine than for anyone to see it. It is better for the truth to be spoken than for any to believe it. Scripture says, "Let God be true, and every man a liar."

Many voices, religious and otherwise, would agree that we are living "in the twilight of a spent civilization."

If God has a word to say to us, now would be a good time to say it. In our day God is speaking again. When I speak to you in the Name of the Lord, God is speaking.

It belongs to your humility as well as to mine that it should be so. Let it also be a cause of joy among us, for thus and not otherwise is the Word of God renewed from generation to generation among his people.

Do you come here expecting to hear a Word from God for our times? If not, why come? You will find better entertainment in the artificial world of television. You will find better entertainment in sleeping late and being quiet.

We do not come here to pay our religious respects. We come here to submit to the Lord God. Indifference or insolence can be disastrous in a setting where judgment and mercy are being offered.

God is speaking. Do you hear what he is saying to you and to our generation?

Surely, this world and its present form is passing away. Perhaps we are making the transition to a new age of the old European civilization. Perhaps European civilization is passing away altogether, only to be replaced by a new civilization. Perhaps we are indeed at the end of all things.

From the still center of our swirling world we should expect the Lord our God to speak. Here! To us! But not only here, not only to us. He does speak. The incarnate Word, Jesus, speaks through his servant. God is speaking. Who in our day is listening?

"If all I had to do was teach a Bible lesson on Jeremiah 1," says Bowen Matthews, "the text would be all I need. But if I am to have a word from God for my congregation, I can never be content with a Bible lesson. There must be something fresh, contemporary, urgent, relevant." That comment sums up the tension of biblical preaching. While the sermon must come from the Scriptures and be faithful to them, it is addressed to men and women struggling in the twentieth century.

Most well-designed sermons start in the present, contemporary world. This sermon does not. Matthews begins 589 years and more before Jesus Christ. Sermons begun in the ancient world sometimes fail to make it into the modern world. They sound like archaeological papers about days long gone by. Yet, Matthews' description of the communications system used in antiquity gets attention, and has a ring of relevance about it. His wording unearths images in the mind, and the listener feels she is learning something. Matthews' wording also bridges the gap between the long ago event and the congregation. New York and Washington are used for comparison. A reference to "the holocaust" pricks the emotions of a sensitive hearer.

The Bible is situated in history. The events took place on a given day in a certain place to particular people. A biblical preacher, therefore, must wear the hat of a historian, and at times, must handle historic information not generally familiar to a modern audience. Because this is the opening sermon on a series from the prophecy of Jeremiah, the background of the book requires an excursion into history. Matthews demonstrates that with thought and creativity the preacher can make dry bones live.

While preaching is basically a monologue, sensitive preachers hold conversations with their hearers. Matthews asks his audience more than twenty questions. Nearly all his major and minor points are introduced by a question and most guide the listener to look at the biblical text for answers. As Matthews opens up the passage, his development clearly follows the verses in Jeremiah 1. The sermon itself is difficult to outline. On paper it looks something like this:

COMMENTARY

124

I. God called Jeremiah to speak his word to Judah.
   A. He spoke as life in Judah reached a fever pitch.
   B. God was speaking when Jeremiah spoke to the circumstances of his day.
      1. Human circumstances hold divine meaning.
      2. Jeremiah interpreted those circumstances to the people.
   C. God's calling to a ministry involves both feeling and fear.
      1. It is a feeling that God called you before you were born.
      2. It is a fear that you are not qualified for the task.
II. The message of a true prophet demonstrates God's call.
   A. His message is reliable.
   B. His message judges our sin.
   C. His message meets with opposition.
III. Whenever God's Word is spoken, we must listen.
   A. Many refuse to listen and reject the truth.
   B. The truth is spoken so that in humility we can accept it and alter our lives by it.

The sermon follows an inductive development which means that the basic idea does not get stated clearly until the final moments. Inductive sermons have an element of surprise and discovery, but they require strong bridges between the major points. In addition, they must also have attentive, thoughtful listeners. If the people in the pew fail to carry their end of the experience, or if the transitions are not clear, the preacher and the congregation will not arrive at the conclusion together. In this sermon the development of the idea sometimes loses out to the discussion of the details of the passage. Since the idea is not stated early in the sermon, nor is the subject presented in the introduction, it is not always clear how the individual parts of the development will relate to the overreaching idea of the message.

The conclusion of an inductive sermon brings the idea to its intended destination or else it is a journey to nowhere. Unlike a deductive sermon which primarily reviews what has been said, the conclusion of an inductive sermon is the one place where the whole sermon must come together. Since Matthews asks many different questions throughout his presentation, it is not easy to determine until his conclusion the one central question he is raising and answering. While his conclusion does not spell out in specific detail what a hearer should do in response to God's Word, the implications are not unclear or vague. Some sermons are stronger if a congregation leaves with questions still unresolved.

Here is a sermon that appears to break the rules of homiletics taught by formula but nevertheless holds attention and communicates an important biblical concept. Matthews demonstrates that rules may often be ignored when the preacher has a basic sense of form.

How long does it usually take you to prepare a message?

About twenty to thirty hours a week. I block out twenty hours a week for sermon preparation in my Tuesday through Friday schedule. In addition, I read at night. I'm up early in the morning. I used to do work on Saturday. Sometimes I even do work on Sunday afternoon on a message that may have nothing to do with the next Sunday.

How long did it take you to prepare the message you submitted?

I spent more time on that particular sermon because it was the first in a series.

How long are your sermons?

About twenty-five to thirty-five minutes. That's a long time for people to sit still, and I've just never strayed far from that time frame.

How does your preparation for Sunday morning differ from Sunday evening?

It differs in several respects. I have a much larger crowd in the morning and, therefore, I feel a greater responsibility to be better prepared. But more important, I quite often am more relaxed, more ad lib on Sunday evening. I'm more likely to use something I've preached before, but, of course, rework it for the immediate situation that our church is in. I don't spend twenty to thirty hours in preparation for Sunday night.

How do you develop the biblical content of your sermons?

First, I follow the logical flow of the text. I try to read through the passage. The paragraphs in the discursive literature like Romans or the episode in a narrative passage is my basic unit of study. I seldom get down to only a sentence. Even if I preach a sermon on a verse or two, I try to put that in that larger context of paragraph or episode so that it isn't divorced from the context. I am committed to be faithful to what the text says. Second, I pay attention to what jumps off the page at me as I read and think and pray. Sometimes it's a word, sometimes a human emotion or a relationship. Somehow I see myself, or I see life as I know it, congruent with the text. What comes off the page at me is what I pay close attention to and develop as I work through the sermon process.

When do you use commentaries?

I use commentaries in the preparatory study before I begin writing sermons. They provide information about customs, language, and pertinent theology. Reading a commentary helps me to come at the text with a fuller understanding of its background. Once I start actually writing the sermons, I tend to stay away from commentaries unless there is a particular point I found helpful and I need to go back and review it. But commentaries do not shape sermons. They simply fill my mind and my soul with information and emotions and other helpful data that will be a pool from which I draw as I think about the people I'm going to share this with.

Do you use the original languages regularly?

Well, that depends on what you mean by "regularly." In preparation for next year, I've been reading in the Book of Acts, and I will refer to the Greek text. When I did the sermon on Jeremiah, I read all of Jeremiah in Hebrew. There's some tough Hebrew in there. I wasn't looking for a jewel under every verb or every piece of Hebrew grammar and syntax. I simply wanted to hear and understand the Hebrew words that Jeremiah used. It contributes to my soul, how I feel the Book of Jeremiah. Much of Jeremiah was written in poetry. He repeated words, but the English translation may have used different words. Jeremiah used the same word again and again. Robert Alter, in his book *The Art of Biblical Narrative,* believes that words and ideas that are repeated are clues to the author's meaning.[1] In the original language, I see that more clearly. So, yes, I use original languages, but I don't think of myself as a scholar.

Where do you get your illustrations?

Anywhere I can. They've got to be interesting and pertinent. I think every preacher has, first of all, an enormous wealth of personal experience that he has gone through or has witnessed in other people. And I find that those things just come bubbling up out of my subconscious. I guess I have tried intermittently to keep card files or some kind of file. I do have a folder in my files that's called "Ideas to be Developed" or "Interesting Things" and I just stick things in there. From time to time I look through it. But most of the time, when I reflect and let things come up out of my subconscious, it's amazing what that produces. If I've heard something or seen something that really is striking and is not in print, I'll often write it out and stick it somewhere where I'll know where to get it when I need it. As you see, I'm not very structured.

How do you develop your introductions?

First, I remember that I'm trying to help distracted people do what they very seldom do—listen to one man talk uninterruptedly for half an hour. Introductions serve to get them with me, to orient us for what is to come in the text and in its homiletical development. I try to see what's coming up out of my soul into my conscious mind. And then for me, the discipline begins in trying to structure this thing so that those first two to five minutes accomplish three objectives: capture distracted attention, orient us to what's coming, and answer the question, "Why should I listen to you?" I seldom start by reading Scripture or asking people to open the Bible. I usually start with something from our common experience. It's helpful to keep people guessing. That's one more way to capture wandering minds for a few minutes. I try not to be predictable. I don't want my people to walk into the sanctuary

1. Robert Alter, *The Art of Biblical Narrative* (New York: Basic Books, 1981), p. 91.

thinking, "I know how he's going to start the sermon." They never know.

Why do you spend as much time and strength on your sermons as you do?

That half hour on Sunday morning represents the one time that I have the most exposure to my people. I think it warrants every piece of energy I invest in it. And that's why all the hours and hours and all the reading and all the preparation and all the bubbling out of my subconscious. I think people need it and deserve it.

What was the greatest challenge for you in approaching the biblical text of the sermon on Jeremiah?

There were several challenges. One was relevance. What does the chapter have to do with life as we live it? At first glance, much of the Old Testament seems even more remote from life at first glance than anything in the New Testament. If it does have something to do with life, the second challenge is, how can I convey something of its meaning to our present experience and be interesting in doing it? And third, how can the first sermon in a series as heavy as Jeremiah be given in such a way to make people want to hear more? The worst thing I could think of would be to start a series in September and have people walk away from the first sermon and say, "Oh, good night, you mean he's going to be here for the next eight months?"

Your sermon seems to lack a strong conclusion. Does that bother you?

There's one thing that's not in this printed sermon. It does not have a conclusion in the sense that it lacks an application. What I will do in a sermon typically when I get down to the end is say, "How can we open some doors into our experience so that Jeremiah doesn't seem so far away? What could we do in the next seventy-two hours that might help us to respond to this?" I then give one or two or maybe three very specific things that somebody can do today or tomorrow. It's not written there. I just add it to the end. I don't remember what I added to the end of this sermon because it changes. My conclusion could be different every time I preach Jeremiah. It depends on what I know about the people, what I know about situations in the world. There's no way to predict it. Sometimes as late as five minutes before I preach, something may come to mind that fits. Usually I spend time getting ready for the application, too, but I like to work on it closer and closer to that actual time of the sermon so it's definitely going to pertain to something on people's minds.

Why did you shape your sermon as you did?

The first sermon in a series sets the tone; it awakens interest in what's going to follow. I don't know that this sermon on Jeremiah was typical of all the sermons on Jeremiah I preached. I have a poetic, or deeply emotional, side to my personality that comes out from time to time in the prose I write. I sometimes deliberately write an introduction in poetic meter. I attempt to hide the meter so it doesn't sound like poetry because people are turned off by that sort of thing. But any time I try to write something that begins to express that poetic, or that unknown, wilder side of me, it comes out in language that is going to be more literary.

Back to the question, it seemed appropriate to the content of Jeremiah's ministry in the times in which he lived. The Book of Jeremiah was apparently compiled after Jeremiah's death and the first chapter, whoever wrote it, was written after the destruction of Jerusalem. It reflects the memory that one man had stood before the kings of Judah and warned, "If we don't change our ways, terrible things are going to come to us from the hand of God." He was ignored and the terrible things came. There is a sense of something dramatic and overwhelming having transpired in the history of God's people. All of those things awakened very deep feelings, and they came out in the style of this first sermon. That's what I mean by it being appropriate to the content of Jeremiah's ministry and the times he lived in.

You've asked over twenty questions in the sermon. Is that deliberate?

Probably I do it because I have a skeptical frame of mind and so I question. The questions are usually some I've asked myself and things I would like answered. But I don't set out to write a sermon and ask a bunch of questions. I think it just comes out as an expression of the kind of person I am.

Do you use notes when you preach?

No, I've never used notes. If I have a particularly bland quotation that's long and I can't remember it, I'll type it out and pull it out of my pocket. But I don't even do that very often. I manuscript and write out my sermon and read through it several times before I give it. The parts that are really expressive to me I make sure I know cold, however long it takes.

You prepare your sermons weeks and even months in advance. How do you do this?

I was not always ahead. The first break came in how I used my summer months. I was having much more erratic attendance in the summer because of vacations, so I began to take eight to ten weeks in the summer to preach old sermons. I used my concentrated study time during those weeks to start preparing for the fall. That's how I initially got ahead. Since then, I've tried consistently to begin preparation for September in January. That gives me three to five months of concentrated study and research and then by April or May, I start putting things together for September. Another thing I've introduced into my study time is some study for things I want to preach on some day. If I'm preparing Acts for the fall, for instance, I'm also working on Psalms without knowing when I'll use that study. So I'm always trying to work in some part of the text that's coming up in the next two years. That is basically exegesis, attempting to read the text, beginning to let ideas flow and making notes. So when I come to a time where it seems Psalms would be appropriate to us, I've got some basic work done. That's been a big help.

Chapter 7

For "Wait" Watchers Only!
Luke 1:5–25

George Kenworthy

Dr. George Kenworthy is the senior pastor of Faith Missionary Church, Indianapolis, Indiana. He has taught at Trinity College and Denver Seminary and presently teaches as an adjunct professor at Trinity Evangelical Divinity School.

I haven't been in your world very long, but I have noticed that you are a people who wait, and wait, and wait. You wait in lines at stores. You wait for traffic on streets. You wait for appointments. You wait for Christmas. You wait for your friends who are already fifteen minutes late. You wait and you wait and you wait. And sometimes in your waiting there is that nagging question that gnaws at you on the inside, "Is it worth it?" Is there anything in life that is worth waiting for? You see, I know something about waiting. I am Zechariah, a priest. I spent nearly all of my life waiting. Most of my waiting was waiting for God. As a young man I prayed and I asked God to give me a son. Then I waited, and I waited, and I waited. And quite honestly, I got to the point where I wondered if it was worth waiting any longer. I've come here today because I know that many of you have felt what I did so many years ago. You have been waiting for God. You have waited, and waited, and waited. And now in your heart you are wondering, "Is it worth it?" Does God really care?

Luke tells you in the first chapter of his Gospel, in verse 5, that I lived in the days of Herod. He flatters me by going on to say that I was "upright" and "blameless" in my day. But I now know that for all of my blamelessness, for all of my righteousness, I didn't understand what it meant to "wait for God." God had to teach me that his gifts are worth waiting for. I know that some of you love God as I did. You pray as regularly as I did. There may be people who look at you and say that you are righteous and blameless, just the way they said that about me. But perhaps like me, you have been waiting for God and you are wondering if it is worth waiting anymore. I would like to tell you my story. It is found in Luke 1:5–25. Through the experience that Luke describes, God taught me that his gifts are worth waiting for. There are three gifts in particular that are worth waiting for.

The first is the gift of *knowing God's purpose.* You see from the passage in Luke that I was a priest, according to the order of Abijah. In my day, all of the descendants of Aaron were priests. There were some twenty thousand priests who served God throughout Palestine. These priests were divided into twenty-four courses or divisions. Mine was the course of Abijah. There were probably about a thousand priests in my division alone. Because there were so many of us, we didn't all serve in the temple at the same time. We all would go down to Jerusalem during the time of the Feast of Pentecost, the Feast of Tabernacles, and the Feast of Passover. But for the rest of the year we served God throughout Palestine. Each course then went down to Jerusalem to serve for two weeks, one week at a time.

As my story begins it was our week to be in Jerusalem serving God. One priest every morning and every evening had the privilege of going into the temple to offer incense on behalf of the people of God. The lot was cast. I had about one chance in a thousand of being called. There was no good reason for me to expect to win the lottery, but I did! I know that you may not understand the significance of this, since all of this priestly service is somewhat foreign to you, but you need to know that this was a once-in-a-lifetime experience. I was thrilled! For me it was better than winning a state lottery. I went into the temple to offer incense on behalf of the people of Israel. I bowed in my place.

I was saying my prayers to God, burning incense before him, when suddenly I had the feeling that I was not alone. I looked up. There was an alien being standing there. His extraterrestial eyes bored right through me. I was terrified. When I went into the temple, I did not expect to have a "close encounter of the frightening kind"! And then the intruder looked right at me and said:

> Do not be afraid, Zechariah; your prayer has been heard. Your wife Elizabeth will bear you a son, and you are to give him the name John. He will be a joy and delight to you, and many will rejoice because of his birth, for he will be great in the sight of the Lord. He is never to take wine or other fermented drink, and he will be filled with the Holy Spirit even from birth. Many of the people of Israel will he bring back to the Lord their God. And he will go on before the Lord, in the spirit and power of Elijah, to turn the hearts of the fathers to their children and the disobedient to the wisdom of the righteous—to make ready a people prepared for the Lord.

SERMON

137

In that moment I knew that God cared for me. You see, all of my life I had been coming before God seeking his purpose. All of my life I had been coming before God and praying that God would reveal his will to me. Yet so often I waited, and waited, and waited, and God's face was hidden from me. It was as if the windows of heaven were locked shut as I prayed. Now in that moment I knew that it was worth waiting to know the plan of God. Because as that angel stood before me and said, "Don't be afraid, Zechariah; your prayers have been heard," I knew that God cared for me; I knew that he was interested in me; and I understood what it means to worship God. I understood what it means to come into his presence, and know that my fear can be taken away, that my disappointment can be eliminated, that I can know that there is a Father in heaven who hears when I pray.

I've come here today because I know that many of you have prayed as I've prayed. You have bombarded heaven with your prayers. You have prayed and prayed and prayed that somehow God would reveal his will to you. But it is as if the heavens are closed and God's face is hidden from you. You have waited and waited and waited, and you wonder now if it is worth it. Let me encourage you. God does want to give you the gift of knowing his purpose. God is concerned about you as he is concerned about me. No matter what the trials and the circumstances of your life are, no matter how frustrated you may be in your waiting, God wants you to know his plan. God wants you to know that he cares. The question that God asks you today is, "Are you willing to wait?" Are you willing to wait for the gift of knowing his purpose?

God gives good gifts to those who wait. God showed me that he desired to give me the gift of knowing his purpose. But also God showed me that he wanted to give me the gift of *realizing his promise.* Luke tells you in verse 17 of chapter 1 that a great promise was fulfilled in my day. The promise had been given by the prophet Malachi. It is found in Malachi 4:5–6, the very last verses of the Old Testament. That's where God says, "I will send you the prophet Elijah before that great and terrible day of the LORD comes. He will turn the hearts of the fathers to their children, and the hearts of the children to their fathers; or else I will come and strike the land with a curse." For four hundred years we waited for that promise. We waited for the revival to happen and for four hundred years it did not happen.

In my day we desperately needed a revival. In verse 5 Luke says that I lived in the days of Herod. The Herod about whom Luke is speaking was Herod the Great. Herod the Great was an Idumean, that is to say, he was an Arab and a Jew. You can picture the difficulty that this would cause by imagining Yasser Arafat being both a Jew and an Arab. It was a political nightmare. Herod the Great tried everything he could to please both the Jews and the Arabs. He built a beautiful temple for the Jews. I believe that Herod's temple was more awe-inspiring and ornate than the Sistine Chapel and your Crystal Cathedral combined! However, we priests were very disturbed by the fact that Herod also had built temples for the pagan idols throughout the land of Palestine. Although he was concerned to appease us somewhat as we talked about our religious concerns, he also encouraged immorality. He had ten wives. He didn't see anything wrong with polygamy. He even tried to impose his polygamous ways on all of us. What's worse, he ordered the strangulation of two of his sons because they didn't agree with him. A third he had executed. Even Augustus Caesar said, "It is better to be Herod's hog than to be his son." We needed a revival in my day. Jews all around me were turning from God, living in sin and acting as though God didn't care. And those of us who believed in God prayed for revival. We prayed for that prophecy of Malalchi to come true. We prayed that we would see the day when the hearts of fathers would be restored to their children, and the hearts of children to their fathers. We waited, and waited, and waited for that promise, but it didn't come. And to be perfectly honest, I had come to the point where I was seriously wondering if I should even preach that promise anymore.

I have come here today because I know that many of you here are praying for revival. Many of you here realize that you live in a day just like mine, where the hearts of fathers need to be turned to their children and the hearts of children need to be turned to their fathers. This is a day when people need to turn to God because of the x-rated values that are propelling your nation headlong into a sewer that reeks with the foul odor of relativism and hedonism. Some of you have been praying that God would do something special in your own home. You've prayed and you've waited, and you've waited, and you've waited. And you've wondered if the promise of God is true anymore. You wonder if your waiting is worth it. I'm here to tell you, "It's worth the wait." God has promised that he will turn the hearts of children to parents, and hearts of parents to children. God has promised that there is a day yet coming, when there will be a revival that will sweep the entire earth and hearts will be renewed before God. There will be a day when God will usher in the new age. God sent his Messiah in my day and he will send his Messiah again. Someday we will be able to live with him for all eternity in joy and happiness. There will be a time without tears, a time of joy. I believed that promise. But God had to teach me the hard way that I didn't believe enough. Perhaps you want to believe that promise, too, but you have waited so long that you wonder if you can claim it anymore. God's promises are true! The question that God asks you is, "Are you willing to wait?"

God had to show me that he was willing to give the gift of knowing his purpose if I would only wait. God had to show me that he would give me the gift of realizing his promise if I could only wait. And finally, God had to show me that he would give me the gift of *experiencing his power* if I would only wait. When the angel Gabriel told me that I was to have a son, I couldn't believe it. I asked, "How can I know that this will be true?" As a priest I had the responsibility of teaching the Torah. All of us priests did. We were to teach the first five books of Moses wherever we were. People would gather as we talked about the great stories in the Bible. I had taught God's people about the miracle of God delivering our ancestors from Egyptian bondage. I had taught God's people about the miraculous birth of Isaac to Abraham and Sarah, even though they were old. I had taught God's people what Abraham said when he was told that God was going to do a miracle for him. He said what I said, "How will I know that this will be true?" In that moment when the angel rebuked me for my disbelief, I suddenly realized that it was far easier for me to pray for a miracle than to believe that one could happen. It was far easier for me to get down on my knees and pray and pray and pray that somehow the power of God would come into my life, than to trust and believe that there is a God in heaven who can turn the key that ignites the power train in my life.

I am here today because I know that many of you are just like me. Maybe it is easy for you to pray for God's power, but a lot harder to believe it. You may want to trust that somehow God is going to do something special for you, but it is hard to believe that that can be true. The great prayer burden of my life was my prayer for a son. I don't know what your great prayer burden is. Maybe you have been praying for your family. Maybe you have been praying for your ministry, or you have been praying about that sin that continually defeats you. You have prayed for an explosion of God's power in your life. Yet, you have waited, and waited, and waited so long, that if the angel of God came to you and said "God has answered your prayer," you would say what I said, "How can this be? How can I know that it is true?" Because for you, as for me, it is easier to pray for a miracle than to believe and to trust that God wants to create that miracle in your life.

Because of my disbelief God took away my ability to speak. For nine long months I contemplated what the angel Gabriel told me. "You will be silent and not able to speak until the day this happens, because you did not believe my words, which will come true at their proper time." For nine months I was forced to endure the judgment of God because I did not have the faith to wait for God's "proper time."

Then after nine months my son was born. All of our friends were rejoicing with us at this marvelous demonstration of God's power in our lives. Our friends assumed that we were going to name our boy Zechariah. Elizabeth said, "No! He is to be called John." Our friends couldn't believe it. No one in our family was called John. They knew it would be an insult to me and my family not to have my son named after one of our relatives. They came to me and asked me what we really wished to name my son. Taking a tablet I wrote, "His name is John." My friends were amazed. Elizabeth and I were not following the practice of our day. We were breaking the tradition of our people, but had no choice. God himself through the angel Gabriel told us that we must name our son John. John is an abbreviation of *Jehohanan,* which means "the gift of God," or "God is gracious." In my wait-ing that is what God wanted to teach me. He is gracious to those who wait on him. As if to confirm that lesson, it was only when I indicated that my son's name would be John, "the gift of God," that God showed his power again by allowing me to speak.

I suppose I was a righteous priest. I suppose that it could be said that I was blameless. But I know as I reflect back on my story that for all of my righteousness, for all of the time that I had spent worshiping God, I hadn't come to that place where I knew what it means to wait for the gifts of God. God had to teach me the importance of being willing to wait for the gift of knowing his purpose. I had to learn that God cared for me enough to demonstrate that the windows of heaven could be opened just

SERMON

141

for me. I had to wait for the gift of realizing God's promise, even though I was living in an immoral age, where sin and sickness were multiplying all around me like maggots. I needed to be willing to wait for the gift of God's promise and to believe that God's Word is true. And I needed to be willing to wait for the gift of experiencing God's power. I needed to believe that as I was praying for God's power in my life, God wanted to show that power to me, if I'd only be willing to wait for what he would do.

I know that many of you feel that you have been wasting a lot of hours waiting. You have grown impatient in your waiting. Some of you have come to the place where you are wondering if you should even be waiting for God anymore. God sent me here to encourage you, to challenge you to believe that the waiting is worth it.

SERMON

142

There is a man who lived in your century, who wrote a poem that I think very appropriately fits what God wants to teach us all today about the "treasure" available to those who wait on him. In his poem he says:

> I wasted an hour one morning beside a mountain stream,
> I seized a cloud from the sky above and fashioned myself a dream,
> In the hush of the early twilight, far from the haunts of men,
> I wasted a summer evening, and fashioned my dream again.
> Wasted? Perhaps. Folks say so who never have walked with God,
> When lanes are purple with lilacs or yellow with goldenrod.
> But I have found strength for my labors in that one short evening hour.
> I have found joy and contentment; I have found peace and power.
> My dreaming has left me a treasure, a hope that is strong and true.
> From wasted hours I have built my life and found my faith anew.[1]

---

1. Taken from Tim Hausel, *When I Relax I Feel Guilty* (Elgin, Ill.: David C. Cook, 1979), p. 67.

In passing judgment on a new book, a reviewer clapped
with only one hand when he wrote, "This book is both scholarly and original. Unfortunately, where it is scholarly it is not
original, and where it is original it is not scholarly." The same
verdict might be handed down about many sermons. Where
they are biblical they are not relevant, and where they are
relevant they are not biblical.

One reason that expository sermons sometimes seem as
out-of-date as running boards on automobiles is that they never
change form. Preachers assume that sermons take only one
shape and that no matter what genre the biblical writers use,
the preacher must refashion it as a sermon. Clyde Fant speaks
to a mindset many preachers picked up in seminary. Their
training, he observes:

> Merely furnished them with a set of homiletical cookie cutters
> which they routinely mash down upon the dough of the text,
> and presto! out pops a little star, or a tree, or a gingerbread
> man.... No matter that the text doesn't want to go into these

forms; the poor thing is mashed and tortured until it is made
to say the things it never intended to say.[2]

In the past, a study of form has been essential to the proper
understanding of a Scripture text; seldom did that form con-
tribute to the shaping of the sermon. Preachers assumed that
the rhetorical tradition planted in Greek and Roman rhetoric
had been given on Mount Sinai or by the apostles rather than
Aristotle. Yet, as a point of fact, no inspired sermonic form
exists. Fred Craddock speaks to this when he says: "Even though
that rhetoric [from Geece] dominated the field of homiletics
for centuries, not even that pattern for oral presentation can
justifiably be called *the* form of a sermon. It remains the case
to this day that a sermon is defined more by content and purpose than by form."[3]

While we must distinguish between content and form, we
must also understand that content and form are never completely separate. Content is shaped by the form it takes. When
an expositor changes the form through which truth was trans-
mitted in the Scripture, she must explain why that change was
necessary or at least be aware that an important structural
change has taken place.

The dramatic monologue, one form a sermon takes, presents
the biblical content from the perspective of a biblical character. This person steps into the modern world out of the
Scriptures and addresses a congregation directly. The first-
person narrative has the flavor of a personal testimony through
which the listeners experience what the individual in the Bible
must have felt. It has the additional advantage of lifting a story
out of the shadowy past and telling it in a concrete, specific,
modern way that allows the audience to meet a biblical character face to face.

George Kenworthy has taken the narrative about Zechariah,
a priest and father of John the Baptist, which Luke relates in

2. Clyde Fant, *Preaching for Today* (New York: Harper & Row, 1975), p. 110.
3. Fred Craddock, *Preaching* (Nashville: Abingdon, 1985), p. 170.

the third person, and forms it into a first-person narrative. In doing so, he keeps the human interest in the story as Luke told it and, at the same time, ties it in a personal way to his congregation. A first-person narrative does not provide any short-cuts in preparation. To be done with integrity, the passages in which the character appears must be examined to discover the author's purpose in writing about him. In addition, the politics, history, geography, setting, and context of the book must be considered for the coloring they give to the life and times of the individual. Only an intensive study of these various backgrounds in the text will guard an expositor from reading into the Bible what is not there and turning imagination into fanciful subjectivity.

Kenworthy delivered this narrative on the Sunday immediately before Christmas. It represents one of his first attempts at giving this type of sermon. The preacher has actually disguised a traditional sermon and dressed it up as the confession of Zechariah. Three abstract points derived from Luke's account are placed into the mouth of Zechariah so that the ancient priest, instead of the preacher, delivers the sermon. The sermon builds on the idea, "God's gifts are worth waiting for," and it makes three easily discernible parallel points.

   I. If we wait, we can know God's purpose.
  II. If we wait, we can realize God's promise.
 III. If we wait, we can experience God's power.

The biblical material appears in the mouth of Zechariah very much as it would in an ordinary sermon. (Zechariah even refers to chapter and verse in Luke's Gospel.) Usually, in a first-person narrative, the inclusion of the scriptural material appears in more subtle and indirect ways. The customs and background of the priesthood and how it functioned in the first century appear easily and naturally in the monologue, but would not differ much from the same information in a didactic presentation. In the mouth of Zechariah, though, the customs take on interest and warmth. The preacher does not simply relate these facts; he actually relives them.

Application presents a special challenge in the first-person narrative. Often it is done indirectly and by implication so that the listener must do a great deal of the work. In this sermon, however, the application is as direct as in an ordinary sermon. Zechariah presses home the points to the congregation very much as though he were a preacher serving in the twentieth century. The audience accepts this since Zechariah has entered our world to give his account of the events and, therefore, it is natural for him to address the people directly.

The people who heard George Kenworthy deliver this first-person monologue responded to it with enthusiasm. The sermon serves as a model that demonstrates how a preacher may begin to try out this form. Take an ordinary sermon developed from a narrative in the Scripture and deliver the sermon through the lips of a central character in the passage. If it is told with empathy and imagination, a minister can recapture the drama of the event as it first occurred and touch the experience of the people by planting theology deep in life.

COMMENTARY

146

How long does it usually take you to prepare a message?

On the average, I spend fifteen to twenty hours in preparation.

How long did it take you to prepare the message you submitted?

It probably took me that amount of time to prepare the sermon on Zechariah.

How long are your sermons normally?

That varies. Before coming to Indianapolis, my messages were about thirty-five to forty minutes in length. But given the fact that here we have three Sunday morning services on top of one another, I now preach only about thirty minutes each time on Sunday mornings.

How do you go about preparing your sermons?

First, generally six months in advance, I determine what my preaching series will be. I've established a goal to preach the whole counsel of God. To make that goal measurable, I balance what I'm doing biblically. If I've been preaching for a period of time in the Old Testament, I have my next series in the New Testament. If I've been preaching on the psalms, I may balance that by preaching on a narrative. In addition,

I try to choose my sermons by determining what the needs of the congregation are.

What steps do you follow in your actual preparation?

Once I've done the preliminary planning, I decide on the series to preach over the next six to twelve months. For example, if I'll be preaching for fifteen weeks on the Gospel of Mark, I lay out the preaching segments of that book. I try to determine the purpose of each individual message, the basic idea of the text, and I give it a preliminary title. Then with the series in mind, I keep an eye out for illustrations and other materials I can use to develop the messages. It's at least a six-month process.

What do you do the week before you actually preach a sermon?

On Monday I am in my Greek or Hebrew Bible, going through the text in the original language. I look up Greek or Hebrew words and do my own translation of the text. Then I look at commentaries. I read exegetical commentaries, but I also read a number of practical commentaries as well, and I look at whatever homiletical material I can get my hands on. I use Bible dictionaries, Bible encyclopedias, Kittel's *Theological Dictionary of the New Testament*[4] to develop the background of the passage. In the process of all this reading, I'm confirming the central idea of the text and the focus of the biblical writer. I'm also in an intensive search for illustrations to use in my sermon.

Where do you get your illustrations?

I find the exegetical work reasonably easy. Finding the right illustration is the challenge. I read contemporary preachers. In addition, I use personal illustrations. I try to think about what has happened in my own life to illustrate a point. As I prepare, I ask myself, "What does God want me to do?" "What have I done in the past and how have I responded to a particular biblical truth in my life?" I find illustrations through that. I read the newspaper carefully. I try to keep up with some popular magazines. I read secular books, and I listen to tapes, all in search of supporting materials.

4. Gerhard Kittel and Gerhard Friedrich, eds., *Theological Dictionary of the New Testament,* ed. and trans. Geoffrey W. Bromiley, 10 vols. (Grand Rapids: Eerdmans, 1964–1976).

What about introductions to your sermons? How do you think about them?

An introduction should establish a sense of need. So, I ask myself, "To what extent does my congregation feel the need to hear what I have to say to them?" Some messages are going to be home runs because the audience feels a need for them. They need help in their marriages, in rearing their children, or in struggling with anger. Those messages are easy to introduce because people are eager to hear them. But there are other messages in which my audience does not sense a pressing need. They don't usually feel a need for a message on evangelism or the sovereignty of God. Developing introductions to those subjects presents more of a challenge for me. I try to draw my congregation into those messages with an illustration that points up the importance of what I'm preaching, or I'll try to find a startling quote that shocks the people into listening to what I'm going to say.

What else do you aim at in your introductions?

Of course, I also want to introduce the subject of my message and somehow orient the audience to the biblical text.

What was the greatest challenge for you in approaching the biblical text of this sermon on Zechariah?

To tell this very familiar story in a way so that anyone familiar with the Bible would want to hear it. I've discovered that the first-person narrative approaches Christmas messages or other familiar passages from a fresh perspective.

How comfortable were you in preaching that kind of sermon? What did you feel as you did it?

For fifteen years, I did not include first-person narrative sermons in my repertoire. But, as an assignment for a seminar at Denver Seminary, I did this first-person narrative. I felt very uncomfortable doing it the Sunday I preached. After I finished, I didn't have a sense of satisfaction, just relief that it was over.

What reaction did your congregation have to the sermon when you delivered it?

I had fully intended on preaching one first-person narrative sermon to fulfill the requirement for the course and never do one again, but my congregation would not permit it. They encouraged me to do another one. I was still uncomfortable with it. I am not particularly dramatic or gifted to do this type of sermon, but, each time I've given one, the audiences have responded positively. More important, they have been able to see biblical truths in ways that they had never seen them before.

Do you use first-person narratives often?

I tend to use them at holidays. Because of the unique challenges I face with preaching at Christmas and, because of the pageantry of that time of the year, Christmas is a very natural time for me to do a first-person narrative.

What is the most helpful skill that you learned from your Doctor of Ministries seminars on preaching?

How to communicate one central truth! I previously loaded up my spiritual shotgun and blasted my listeners with all the details that I had unearthed in my study of a passage. It was difficult for anyone to pick out one clear idea that came from the text.

Also, in the past, my messages focused a lot more on what happened in the first century or in the eighth century B.C. than on the twentieth century. The homiletics seminar helped me develop twentieth-century outlines and to present biblical truth in a way that a listener can understand how God wants him to apply truth to his life today.

Finally, I developed a new appreciation for word pictures and how to tell illustrations so that people picture what you are saying.

Chapter 8

Who Cares?
Luke 15

Joseph M. Stowell

Dr. Joseph M. Stowell is the president of Moody Bible Institute. He is the author of *Tongue in Check, Kingdom Conflict, Through the Fire,* and *Fan the Flame.* He served as senior pastor at Highland Park Baptist Church in Southfield, Michigan, for ten years.

"Who cares?"

I was surprised by my reaction to the yellow diamond-shaped sign hanging in the back window of the car in front of me. In context the statement seemed insensitive and cold.

It's not that I'm against commuter communication. I'm an unrepentant fan of clever bumper stickers. I still laugh when I think of the sticker that boasts, "As a matter of fact I do own the road!"

The addition of yellow signs to our bumper talk has made driving more fun. It all started with the sober warning, "Baby on board." Soon we added, "Ex-boyfriend in trunk" and "Nobody on board." But the sign that said, "Who Cares?" in response to the "Baby on board" warning seemed tragic, not funny. What is more precious, more helpless, more special than a baby? If there is anything we should care about, it's infants. Anyone with the slightest parental instinct would recoil at the thought of not caring about babies.

If God were into commuter talk, he would hang yellow signs around the necks of those who are without Christ that say, "Precious to God." Would we then be seen with signs that proclaim, "Who Cares?"

The lost are the traffic in our lives. They are our neighbors, friends, and family. They are associates at work, enemies, criminals, and kings. The issue before us is not knowing their presence, but measuring our response. When was the last time you felt compassion for the lost? Prayed for the lost? Reached out in a concrete way to touch the lost for Christ? Do we care? Or, do we care less for the lost?

A "care-less" response to the lost places us in awkward company, with strange bedfellows indeed. In Christ's day, the religious leaders, the Pharisees, had a "Who Cares" attitude toward the sinner.

One of the most penetrating and instructive revelations of their attitude toward sinners occurs in Luke 15, where they arrive with their "Who Cares" signs in full view. In response, Christ tells three stories. They have become classics. They are the parables of the lost lamb, the lost coin, and the lost son. More important than an appreciation for his masterful presentation is an understanding of the purpose and setting in which they were spoken. Christ told these stories to confront and reprove the Pharisees for murmuring about the fact that he spent time with those who were lost.

The text reads:

> Now the tax collectors and "sinners" were all gathering around to hear him. But the Pharisees and the teachers of the law muttered, "This man welcomes sinners and eats with them." (Luke 15:1–2)

The parables that comprise the remainder of the chapter are born out of the tension in verses 1 and 2 between the muttering Pharisees and the evangelistic efforts of Christ. Through these three stories, Christ seeks to correct the attitude of the Pharisees. We can expect that they will correct us as well and stimulate our hearts to be at one with his.

In essence, the theme that is woven through each parable is that God cares enough for the tax collectors and sinners to seek and to save them. If we are asking, "Who cares?" then the resounding answer in this text is that God cares. And since God cares, the text carries profound implications in regard to our own caring as well.

Christ teaches us that to be found in the nonreligious crowd as a seeker of souls is not a contradiction to godliness. He wants to draw us from the pharisaical fringe to the core of the crowd with him.

With the theme of this three-act play in hand, let's introduce the identity of the players. The shepherd, the woman, and the forgiving father represent God. Christ seeks to correct the Pharisees' theology. It is his intention to change their bent notions of God.

The lost sheep, the lost coin, and the lost son each portray the lost, unregenerate sinner. It is Christ's intention to challenge the Pharisees' false perceptions of the lost.

The elder son in the third parable is cast as a stunning reproof to the grace-less, care-less Pharisees.

Christ masterfully casts the players and writes the script to make his point. Caring for the lost is a divine priority. If we are to be like God, it is necessary to reach out to touch them. The proof of our caring as God cares is where we are found. Are we murmuring at the fringe of the crowd, or rejoicing with Christ in the pursuit and salvation of the sinner?

Three vitally important truths in our text challenge and re-order our response to the lost. First, some cultural and theological background will help us understand the roots of a *care-less correctness* that, like the Pharisees, may be the very reason that we care less for the lost. Then Christ introduces through the parables a *divine correction* of our misperceived correctness. Third, the stories provide a clear three-step pattern of *applied compassion* for the lost.

We learn from this chapter that *caring requires a correction that produces compassion.*

Why would religious people, to say nothing of leaders, have such disregard for the lost? The fact that they cared less for the lost than Jesus did grows out of a cultural and theological bias that led them to a false perception of their own "correctness."

Culturally, in the context of their religious rules and perspectives, it was not correct for godly people to associate with "tax collectors and sinners." It was especially reprehensible to eat with them. Eating together in Christ's day was a token of acceptance and a statement of relationship. You could be implicated by the company you ate with. The fact that Christ welcomed and ate with sinners was repugnant to the cultural mores of the religious establishment—so much so that the Pharisees used this statement to discredit his claim to be God. If he were God, he wouldn't mix with that crowd.

But in their perceived correctness they couldn't have been further from the truth. They cared less because they were molded by false religious perceptions. They were culturally correct, but morally wrong.

This cultural "correctness" grew out of a false sense of theological correctness. Why would they not mix with the masses? Because their theology, though seemingly orthodox, was tragically mistaken.

The Pharisees held a "good guys–bad guys" view of theology. Good guys keep the law and bad guys don't. God loves the good guys and hates the bad. In their view, no amount of judgment would be enough for the sinner. They knew plenty about justice and little of mercy and grace. They knew nothing of the view that evangelism is simply one beggar telling another beggar where to find bread. Therefore, it was a theological contradiction for this one who claimed to be God to linger with the lost.

What they perceived to be culturally and theologically correct isolated them from the masses. No wonder they murmured from the fringes when they saw Christ at the core of the crowd. Their "correctness" made it impossible to process the statement, "I have come to seek and to save that which is lost."

We are not exempt from having our concern for the lost victimized by similar dynamics. The retail store where I worked as a seminary student threw a gala banquet. When I arrived, my fellow clerks and salespeople were mingling with cocktails in hand. I must admit that I felt immediate discomfort. I got that old "what's a nice boy like you doing in a place like this" feeling.

I thought about people I knew who would not approve if they saw me. It just wasn't culturally correct. My theology began to issue in questions like "Would Christ come here?" and "Would I want God to find me here?" Since there certainly are some places where Christ wouldn't go and where I would not want God to find me, I wondered if this was one of those places. I was so preoccupied with my cultural and theological "correctness" that I was distracted from the lostness of my friends and the fact that God cared for them and sought them for himself.

Our theologies of grace, predestination, separation, and assurance can, instead of stimulating us to evangelism as they should, produce a sense of apathy and in some cases a murmuring scrutinization of those who are lost and even of those who zealously pursue the lost.

At the close of a service, a young executive came to me and said that the small office staff where he had sought to have an influence for Christ was going to honor his boss with a dinner. The party was to be held in a tavern. He wanted to know if he should go. What would you have said?

Where do we find ourselves in this text? Standing with the Pharisees on the murmuring fringe or with Christ at the core of the crowd?

This text produces not only this personal tension, but probing questions as well. Is it possible to be with sinners and not be a sinner? Is it possible that there is a difference between the decadence of sin and the worth of the sinner? Can I be separated from this world yet be involved in the lives of those who are in the world? How would God respond to the lost?

Christ seeks to correct the misperceived correctness of the Pharisees by making four points about God's perception of the sinner. He answers the question, Why would a holy and just God care for and seek after a sinner?

First, because the lost are a loss to God. When we talk in terms of "the lost" we think of their condition and position before God. Our emphasis is in terms of the lostness of the individual. "Sinners deserve to be lost," says our theology. All three stories affirm that sinners are lost, but more important that their lostness is a loss to God. The shepherd lost a lamb; the woman a coin; the father a son.

I find that I have great concern when something that is precious to me is lost. When I misplace my keys, my money clip, or valuable papers, finding them becomes my priority. Because of sin and the fall, the highest glory of God's creation is lost to him—lost to his purposes, fellowship, and pleasure. Seeking the lost is not a chore to God; it is a heartfelt pursuit. It would be inconsistent if God did not care for and seek the "tax collectors and sinners." They are not just lost; they represent his loss.

Second, because the lost have worth and value to God. Note the choice of symbols in the text. Each of them is a precious commodity. In the day that Christ told these stories, a family's wealth was measured in terms of their flock. It was their bank account. Needless to say, a woman who has only ten silver pieces and loses one has lost something of great value. And what needs to be said about the worth of a son?

Are there any of us who believe that the "righteous" are valuable to God and that sinners are significantly depreciated in his sight? The truth is that sinners are not depreciated in his sight. Those who are lost are worth more attention from us than those who are firmly in place.

The hippie movement in the sixties represented a societal movement of godlessness. Immorality in terms of "free love," drugs, rebellion against authority, and disregard for the Judeo-Christian ethic were the theme songs. As a college student, I had little time for or patience with the movement or its members. I recall pulling onto an interstate and seeing a hippie, disheveled with knapsack and guitar in hand, hitchhiking. As I sped by, self-righteous thoughts filled my mind. "Why doesn't he get a job and buy his own car? Besides, I wouldn't want to travel miles with someone whose philosophy of life is so blatantly pagan."

God interrupted my thoughts. I contemplated how God would have viewed that traveler. I was immediately reproved for my attitude. I knew that God saw through the externals and saw in that hippie someone precious to him. He should have been precious to me as well.

Third, because they are helplessly and hopelessly lost in and of themselves. In spite of the advice that someone gave to Little Bo Peep, lost sheep don't come home by themselves. Lost coins have no ability to find themselves. A son who has so blatantly raped his father's estate has no claim to recovery unless he is received and forgiven by the father.

Paul Harvey reported that the Italian team at the '87 Americas Cup competition in Australia went to the "outback" on a day off to see if they could see a kangaroo in the wild. They had been outfitted by the designer Gucci with jackets, wallets, hand bags, and luggage. To their surprise, near the end of their search, a kangaroo jumped out from the bush and was struck by their jeep. With the kangaroo lying motionless before them, they decided to put the driver's jacket on the animal and take a picture of a Gucci-clad kangaroo. As they stepped back to snap the picture, the kangaroo, who was not dead but merely stunned, jumped up and hopped into the bush wearing the jacket. To the dismay of the crew, the driver's keys and wallet were in the jacket as well.

Christ wants us to know that sinners are not stunned by sin. They are dead in sin. They cannot come to their senses by themselves and hop off clothed in the jacket of Christ's righteousness with the keys to the kingdom in their pocket. Self-reformation before God is no reformation at all. Without God's help, these precious lives are hopelessly, helplessly, and eternally lost.

Fourth, because heaven rejoices in the recovery of the lost. Christ's emphasis in each parable is on the sense of rejoicing and celebration in heaven. This poetical form makes rejoicing the pivotal point of each parable. This is intended by Christ to contrast the murmuring of the Pharisees with the enthusiasm in heaven when the lost are won. If heaven throws a party when the lost are found, what are we doing with the Pharisees at the fringe of the crowd?

Knowing that the lost are a significant loss of that which is precious to God and knowing that these lives are hopelessly and helplessly lost, we should be corrected from our misperceived notions and be found rejoicing with heaven in the finding of the lost. These four pointed truths correct the cultural and theological misconceptions that keep the "Who Cares" spirit alive in our hearts. This divine correction is the prerequisite of our care-less correctness to developing a compassion that places us in the midst of the masses with Christ.

One cannot escape the throbbing sense of compassion that flows through each of these stories. Biblical caring always issues in action. The Bible knows nothing of a compassion that is not busy.

Having understood God's correcting perspective on the lost, we must face the challenge of actualizing a busy compassion toward the sinner. These parables underscore three critical steps that move us to a compassionate response toward those precious lives hopelessly and helplessly lost to God.

First, repent of prejudice. It is not without significance to note the individuals whom Christ chose to be identified as God: a shepherd, a woman, and a father who forgives a son who had violated every Jewish tradition in relationship to his father. Christ chose to represent God as three classes of people that the Pharisees despised. Shepherds were considered lower class and unworthy. Women were of no value to the Pharisees. And to forgive a son like the prodigal was unthinkable. Christ's casting of God in these terms was a shock to the Pharisees, a reproof of their prejudice. In fact, their prejudice against sinners in general was the major roadblock to their ability to truly care for the lost.

We must think carefully before we discount the problem of prejudice among us today. We, too, need reproof.

We send missionaries all over the world. We claim that the mission field is the world. And now the world has moved to our doorstep. If an Indian Hindu, an Arabic Muslim, or even a black moved onto our street, would we thank God for bringing the mission field to our neighborhood, or would we hunt for a good real estate broker before our equity was endangered?

When we think of different ethnic and cultural groups (the poor, sick, yuppies, punkers, rockers, Muslims, Jews, Arabs, blacks, whites, welfare users, drug abusers) do we respond prejudically or evangelistically? Is the gospel only for middle-class blacks and whites, or is it truly a universal message for a universal need?

It's been a long time since we've sung,

> Red and yellow
> Black and white,
> They are precious
> In His sight . . .

We need to sing it again.

Second, accept ownership of the task. Christ clearly implies ownership in each of the parables. From the sheep belonging to the shepherd to the woman's coin to the father's son, evangelism is cast in terms of ownership. In fact, the shepherding parable may imply that seeking the lost is family business. In their day, shepherding was done, for the most part, by family members. And, as we have seen, it was a task delegated to the lowliest family members. Hence, the youngest and least significant member of the family, David, was assigned to the sheep and was not able to meet the great prophet of Israel, Samuel.

Accepting personal ownership of the task may be tough, especially if we are used to being spectators in evangelism. We watch crusades, attend evangelistic meetings, watch invitations, and thrill when the pastor leads someone to Christ. We write checks for others to do it. We are always cheerleaders and supporters, but rarely players.

Christ calls us to accept the task as a matter of personal responsibility in family business. In my first year of seminary, my dad sent me a check for $100.00. That was significant! I promptly misplaced it. How did I respond? Casual detachment? Not on your life. An aggressive, time-consuming, apartment-disrupting search ensued. I accepted personal ownership of a family loss.

We, too, must be about our Father's business.

Repenting of our prejudice and accepting ownership of the task should prepare us to seek the lost. In all my years of ministry I have never heard of anyone coming to the church's lost-and-found to rummage through the lost items out of simple curiosity.

What makes people seek the lost? A personal sense of the loss of something of value.

Applied compassion, then, must include not only a repentant new perspective on the lost and an acceptance of ownership, but applied compassion must reach out to seek the lost.

In the first parable there are four dynamics that comprise an effective seeker of the lost.

The first is *leaving*. The text states, "Suppose one of you has a hundred sheep and loses one of them. Does he not leave the ninety-nine in the open country and go after the lost sheep until he finds it?" Seeking demands leaving—leaving our comfort zones of friends and all that is familiar, leaving our holy huddles where we feel accepted to go into the unknown wilderness of our world. It may cause some discomfort; we may get smoke blown in our face, but there will be little seeking if there is no leaving.

What would you think if someone said that she was missing Sunday evening church or prayer meeting because it was the only night she could have her unsaved neighbors over for dinner? Or, if a friend in your fellowship group didn't show up for potluck because he was out with some friends who didn't know Christ? Bless them! Pray that their tribe might increase. Seekers must be leavers.

The second dynamic is *finding*. Christ continues the story by stating that the shepherd seeks the lost, "until he finds it." Note the sense of persistence in the word *until*. Brief forays into the masses bear little fruit. Persistence pays.

When my dad and I used to fish, we never wanted to get "skunked." That was our term for catching nothing. That meant we stayed at it.

Our first family dog had a terrible bent for running. If we opened the door, he was gone! Our daughter, Libby, had a great love for the dog, Sam. He was precious to her and she accepted ownership of the task. One day she walked out of our subdivision, across a major mile road, through another subdivision, into an open field where finally she found him. Libby was a finder. So are true seekers.

The third dynamic is *bearing*. Christ goes on to say that "when he finds it, he joyfully puts it on his shoulders and goes home."

Little Bo Peep got some jaded advice. She had lost her sheep and someone said, "Leave them alone and they will come home, wagging their tails behind them." Not true. Lost lambs don't come home by themselves. She may still be waiting. Note that this shepherd bore the lamb to the fold.

There may be some bearing for us to do as well. We may need to introduce a new believer to our friends. We may need to disciple them, sit with them in church, or help them sort through the realities of a life where "old things are passed away and behold all things have become new."

Christ implies a continuing sense of responsibility to integrate the lost into the flock. Seekers are bearers.

The fourth dimension is *rejoicing*. As our Libby walked back through our subdivision with Sam firmly in her grasp, she was beaming. Our family was out on the front lawn and all of us started cheering. The lost was found. It was a cause for celebration.

In the text, the shepherd "calls his friends and neighbors together and says, 'Rejoice with me; I have found my lost sheep.' " The woman rejoiced and the father threw a celebration. Heaven rejoices. What a contrast to the murmuring, care-less attitude of the Pharisees.

Many of our lives and churches are characterized by a strange sense of joylessness. For many, religion has become routine. Murmuring seems more prevalent than rejoicing in the Christian community.

One of our sources of joy is the finding of the lost. Without this dynamic, we move closer to a joyless experience in the body of Christ. Could it be that our care-less correctness has exiled rejoicing to little more than a word in our hymnals?

What then is the remedy? It begins with an honest measurement of our own attitude toward the lost. Have we been victimized by a care-less brand of correctness? If so, we must permit God to correct us with his perspective on the lost. This correction sets the stage for an applied compassion that repents of its prejudice, accepts ownership of the task, and seeks the lost.

Caring demands a correction that produces compassion.

It was one of those cold, snowy nights in the heart of the Christmas rush. We had gone with my parents to the huge Wood-field Mall just outside of Chicago to do some browsing and shopping. Suddenly we realized that our little son, Matthew, was missing. Seized by the thought that he may have been victimized by a "mall kidnapper" we had heard so much about, we began to search frantically. I was assigned to the parking lot. As I ran through the snow, I felt foolish as I called, "Matthew! Matthew!" But, I knew that his loss was more important than my pride. I kept running and calling.

He was not to be found.

I went back inside and we regrouped. No one had seen him.

Just then my dad appeared holding Matthew by the hand. We were relieved and full of joy.

Where had he been?

At the candy counter.

Hands behind his back, with the candy right at eye-level, he didn't look lost. He didn't even know he was lost!

But he was, and in great danger at that.

Today, most people don't look lost and, more significantly, they don't know they are lost. The goods, the goals, the glory, and the gusto preoccupy the lost and dull their sense of lostness. Who will be there to reach out to them when the candy is gone, when the allurements of this world prove illusory, when the sound of success rings hollow, when the liberty of the flesh has enslaved, when bountifulness leads to brokenness?

When they know they need the Lord, who will be there? Who will care?

People for the most part don't look lost. They don't feel lost, but they are lost. People need the Lord.

As a boy, I used to fall asleep listening to a late-night New York City broadcast. A warm, deep, tender voice began the show by saying, "Have no fear. 'Big Joe' is here." He would then break into song.

Somebody cares about you
And worries till the sun comes shining through.
Somebody cares if you sleep well at night,
If your day goes all wrong
Or if your day goes all right.
Somebody cares about you
And worries til the sun comes shining through.
Please, believe me, it's so.
But in case you didn't know,
Somebody cares.

There was something wonderful about "Big Joe" to my boyish heart. It must have been a great strength to the lost and lonely lives in that massive city.

The crowd around Christ on that day in Luke 15 must have felt he cared for them. I wonder if the world around me, those who are lost, sense that I am that someone who cares?

People need the Lord.

SERMON

165

The parables fascinate modern biblical scholars as few other types of sacred literature. Yet while seminary library shelves are filled with exegetical and hermeneutical studies on parables, very few of these books provide much assistance to preachers desiring to preach these stories to their people. Although most offer the well-established advice that parables make one central point and so should the preacher, they don't answer a minister's practical question, "How should I go about developing my sermon from a parable?"

Some expository preachers have been so stymied by the parables they have ignored these hearty tales Jesus told! In fact, they believe the profound theology of the Bible can be found only in the letters of Paul, Peter, James, and John. They may unintentionally slight one-third of the teachings of Jesus because it comes wrapped in common, ordinary stories. Even the Apostle's Creed, "He was born of the virgin Mary; suffered under Pontius Pilate...," dismisses Christ's teaching ministry with a semicolon. Yet most preachers value the parables because they appreciate the impact of a well-crafted story. These stories Jesus told may sound at first like pleasant yarns, but they have something up their sleeves which pops out and flattens us.

Expounding a parable resembles playing the saxophone: it is easy to do poorly. A legion of preachers has allegorized these stories, giving undue significance to details in the parable that add nothing but a splash of color. Proponents of the "new hermeneutic" argue that explaining a parable is as futile as explaining a funny story. A parable, like a joke, can only be retold and, therefore, a preacher's task is to retell the parable so that a modern audience will experience what the original hearers felt.

While a great deal can be said in support of "telling the story," parables, like good jokes, can be destroyed in other ways. Colin Morris warns, "The narrative preacher had better be quite sure that he is not doing badly what the Bible has already done well—dragging out at tedious length in colorless speech what Jesus, for example, captured in one gripping anecdote or a few crisp sentences."[1]

Joseph Stowell, therefore, tackles a difficult passage when he preaches on the most familiar of all Jesus' parables, the account of the prodigal son. Actually, the literary unit includes more than the account of a delinquent boy; it takes in the stories of a lost sheep and some lost silver as well. In handling the entire chapter, Stowell focuses on their common purpose. They uncover God's burden for lost people and teach us that those who identify themselves with God must identify with God's concern.

While Stowell's big idea emerges clearly, it sounds a bit awkward in its statement, "Indifference toward lost people is changed by a correction that produces a compassion that acts." An expanded outline elaborates on Stowell's alliterated outline in the sermon and helps us see its development.

I. "Care-Less Corrections": Religious people do not care about the lost because of cultural and theological biases

1. Colin Morris, *The Word and the Words* (Nashville: Abingdon, 1975), p. 121.

that lead them to a false perception of their own correctness.

    A. Culturally, religious people in Jesus' day believed it was not proper for them to associate with "tax collectors and sinners."

    B. Theologically, religious people believed God loves "good guys" and hates "bad guys."

    C. We are not exempt from having our concern for the lost victimized by the same cultural and theological dynamics.

II. "A Divine Correction": Jesus corrects us by demonstrating that a holy and righteous God cares for and seeks after sinners.

    A. Lost people are a loss to God.

    B. Lost people have worth and value to God.

    C. Lost people left to themselves are helpless and hopeless.

    D. When lost people are recovered, heaven rejoices.

III. "Applied Compassion": If we share God's compassion, we will act in compassion toward the lost.

    A. We will repent of our prejudice against sinners.

    B. We will own the task of evangelism.

    C. We will leave our "comfort zone" to seek the lost.

COMMENTARY

This sermon has a strong sense of unity, order, and progress. In his first major point dealing with the background out of which the parable is told, Stowell highlights the reasons why Jesus told about the sheep, the coin, and the boy. In his second point, he works with all three stories to spotlight their central thrust. In his final point, he draws out of the passage how his congregation should respond.

In the introduction to a sermon, a preacher must sometimes choose between clarity and suspense. If the minister aims only at making the unfolding of the message clear, he may give too much away and, in doing so, relax tension. If he opts for suspense, then he must work harder throughout the sermon to make himself clear. Stowell opts for clarity. He not only gives the idea of the sermon but also how he proposes to develop it. As a result, because the development of his sermon is highly predictable, he must achieve tension and maintain interest in other ways.

Stowell draws his hearers into the message by peppering them with questions. He does not answer most of his questions directly, but they accumulate like bee stings to unsettle his hearers and make them grapple with his basic question, "Who cares?"

Stowell maintains attention and sews his sermon to life with illustrations planted throughout the sermon. When a sermon grows out of a biblical story, it should not drift far from specific, concrete material or else it sounds as abstract as a sociological treatise on the physiology of a kiss. Effective communicators ransack life for illustrations, and they find them everywhere. Stowell spotted his on bumper stickers, at dinner parties, in children's choruses and nursery rhymes, by remembering old songs, through his frustration with a misplaced check, and his experience with a runaway dog and a lost child. A retired song writer in Nashville, remarking about country song writer Tom T. Hall, points out what should be true of every preacher: "You know, some folks can go around the globe and never see a thing. Tom can go just down the road and see the whole darn world."

Preachers who introduce an insight from life with "If you'll pardon this personal illustration" ask forgiveness for false guilt. Illustrations incarnate a message and give it the strength of life. Two warnings about anecdotes from a preacher's experience are in order: don't brag. Boasting is as out of place speaking to a hundred as it is talking with a friend. Second, strive for variety: it is the spice of thought, and a sermon is better flavored by stories gathered from several different sources. Stowell's illustrations serve several purposes. They demonstrate that he is human and has a sense of humor and they allow the hearers both to feel and understand his point.

Perhaps his weakest illustration is the one borrowed from Paul Harvey. While it possesses inherent interest, it misses because it makes a positive point negatively. Stories like this tempt us to tell them for their own sake and not for what they illustrate.

Stowell holds interest and stays close to experience by his questions and anecdotes. He finishes with a conclusion which builds to an emotional and psychological climax in the same way: a final moving story and three well-placed questions.

COMMENTARY

171

How long does it usually take you to prepare a message?

A lifetime. The ultimate product really is shaped and formed out of all that you are and all that you bring to that study time. Specifically, it's a hard question to answer because it depends a lot on the text. Some passages are like walking through a cave where there are no lights and the lights come on slowly. Others fall together quite readily. Probably I take twelve to fifteen hours on the sermon I would preach on a Sunday morning.

How long did it take you to prepare the message you submitted?

A little longer because I was doing quite a bit of reading ahead of time for this one.

How long are your sermons normally?

When I was in the pastoral ministry, forty minutes.

How do you go about preparing a sermon?

First, I read through the passage in English texts, usually the King James, the New American Standard, and the New International Version. I read it through several times to get the general sense. Then I seek, from the English, to isolate pivotal phrases (a phrase that I don't understand well, a phrase that is key to the movement of the passage) and work in the original languages on the five or six key phrases I want to attack in the Greek or Hebrew. Of course, I quickly move from isolated phrases into grammatical relationships. Lights come on when I understand grammatical relationships. For instance, tenses, a result clause, nuances of prepositions often establish the flow of the text. When I am handling a parable, I also read to understand the cultural implications of what Christ was talking about. It's important, too, to work in the wider context. The parables are not told in isolation. They are stories that grow out of a particular situation or context of thought. Then I read the commentaries I may not have already consulted about technical matters.

Is most of your preparation primarily aimed at understanding the passage?

No, indeed. I perceive sermon preparation in two phases. One, the skill phase; the other is the creative phase. The skill phase focuses on the exegetical outline. That's the easiest part of sermon preparation. My weakest sermons have been ones I preached when I finished the skill phase and did not take time to let it germinate and, as John Stott says, "take it into the world of real people." It's like fixing a meal. You can buy the groceries and set them on the counter and say, "Okay, there it is." It's quite another thing to get the recipe out and mix the groceries together and put the food on the table. You might even go a step further and make a great, attractive, nourishing feast. My goal is to prepare a meal that's both nourishing and attractive. From time to time, I try for a feast.

Tell us more about that creative phase of preparation.

You've got to have time to be creative. I begin doing my exegesis no later than Monday. Some ministers do it three to four weeks ahead. As a busy pastor, I was never able to accomplish that. For me, the skill stage and the creative stage don't happen sequentially; they happen together. As I do my exegesis, I keep a pad of paper handy and write down creative ideas that come to me. I have to capture the creative thoughts before they leave me. Creative ideas come and I think I'll never forget them, but the next day they're gone.

Do you have any ways to prime the pump to become creative?

It helps me to depict my sermon in pictures with arrows and stick figures. Visualization of my sermon helps me to think clearly, but it also sparks creative thinking. I also think in similes and metaphors. What is this like? This concept is like stars at night, or trees in a forest, or fishing, or missing a putt by a quarter of an inch in a big tournament. What is this like in terms of my audience? What is this like in my life? This leads into the illustrative stage. I begin to recall ways in which I have interacted with this truth. Living metaphors come out of my own experience to throw light on the concept.

What is the most difficult part of the process for you?

To state my main points and the big idea in clever ways that hook the heart. I'm never satisfied. I can always say it better. That is the stressful thing about sermon preparation; you're never done.

What attention do you give to your wording of the sermon?

I refuse to accept tired words. They're like a broken-down car. You can't be a purist about the English language if you're going to be creative. Made-up words might not be in the dictionary, but they make people stop and think.

For example?

Calling materialism "thingishness." Sometimes as I'm preaching, something creative comes to me out of my preparation. Some new way of saying it.

Where do you get your illustrations?

I get a lot of them out of my experience. I have to fight overburdening my sermons with personal illustrations. People identify with them, but they can turn people off if you use them too often or if they glorify the preacher. I try to use personal illustrations that make me transparent. If I use a positive illustration about myself, I put a disclaimer up front like, "I wish I could always be this spiritual." After all, I'm not Mr. Wonderful who has his act all together.

Aside from your own life, where else do you find illustrative material?

Television advertisements are a rich source. I try to glance at the Sunday newspaper before I preach because I may find a headline or story or an ad, and I can say, "In this morning's paper. . . ." That makes my sermon as fresh as it can be. I read books. I borrow other people's stories. A preacher must be a great collector. You must keep your eyes and ears open all the time. I use magazine articles. *USA Today* has great statistics and it identifies trends in our culture.

What questions do you ask as you prepare your introduction?

Does it catch interest? Does it establish the need? Does it orient the audience to the body of the message? I try to start with something that arrests attention and particularly something the audience can identify with. The hardest thing I had to do in the pastoral ministry where I was preaching two or three times a week was to come up with jugular introductions.

When do you prepare your introductions?

I do them last. I try to give the introduction a lot of creative time. Sometimes I've changed my introduction while I'm sitting on the platform.

What are the problems in preaching parables?

Trying to figure out why Christ told the story, the purpose of the parable. A second challenge is to identify the relationships and the dynamics of the drama. In what way does a lost person belong to a father? What relationship did a lost Israelite have with God the Father? You can't make parables walk on all fours, but you have to figure out their main purpose. Parables are meant to drive home a unifying thrust. Another challenge is understanding the culture behind the parables. A parable can hinge on the cultural background.

You used a barrage of questions in this sermon. Do you usually do that?

I find question asking a tremendous communicative tool. As long as the questions aren't pedantic, they keep people involved in the process of the message.

How do you design your sermons?

That's a difficult question to answer. Every sermon gets shaped differently depending on the context, the audience, the type of message. I try to do what is appropriate to the text so that the shape and the flow of the sermon are not inconsistent with the type of message or audience that I'm working with. I believe clarity is my most significant challenge in sermon preparation. Simplicity is one of the great tools of clarity. So at the risk of being repetitive, I restate and rethread my central concept as often as I can.

How has becoming president of Moody Bible Insititute changed your preaching?

My job requires sixty to seventy hours of my time each week and still doesn't get done. I've had to fight for time to study and prepare. My audience is different. The President's Chapel is a gathering of about two thousand people, fourteen hundred of which are students who are idealistic, sometimes cynical, very analytical. They haven't processed enough life yet to give a speaker a little elbow room. They have been gracious to me, and it's been a wonderful experience. But it is a different audience.

Anything else?

When I'm out on the road, it's usually for two or three messages, and then I'm gone. Or maybe in for just one message and then out. When I had a congregation, I had rapport. I knew who they were; they knew me. I find myself now moving in and out of groups teaching the Word of God where I really don't know the audience. So, I've lost a significant comfort zone.

What is the most helpful skill that you learned from your classes in homiletics?

My preaching has been formed a lot by my father, but in seminary I gained a methodology where I could confidently attack a text. That method—verified, affirmed, and proven in my ministry—was unlike any other homiletical concept I'd ever heard. I knew how to get a handle on a text and I was prepared to communicate it. I wish I could preach in ignorance, but I'm always haunted by whether or not I've got the big idea. This "big idea" preaching skill would be the biggest contribution homiletics made to my life.

A Woman Who Came a Stone's Throw from Death
John 8:1 –12

Nancy Hardin

Nancy Hardin, a graduate of Denver Seminary, has an extensive speaking ministry both in Colorado, where she lives, and around the country. Mrs. Hardin helps women study the Scriptures for themselves and teach the Bible to others.

There are some passages in the Bible which good people feel should not be there. One such passage is John 8:1–12. Some scholars who have studied the ancient manuscripts have grave doubts whether this incident was written by John at all and should be included in his Gospel. There are other more squeamish souls who question it in that it deals with a woman taken in adultery, and at first glance seems to picture Jesus as being soft on sexual sin. Yet Jesus was always seen with the wrong people and seemed to be saying the wrong thing. There were folks who took the Sabbath seriously. He didn't seem to. There were people who were uptight about drinking alcohol. That didn't seem to bother him. He was accused of being a glutton and a drunkard. For folks who were very concerned about evil companions, Jesus hung around with the wrong crowd.

The squeamish will have trouble with the whole Bible, but scholars have more legitimate questions. The story came from someplace. It's unthinkable that some scribe who wanted to put Jesus in a good light would have invented an incident like this.

In the context, the question John raised was, "Is Jesus God?" So you'd think a scribe would introduce a story about raising someone from the dead or calling down fire from heaven. In the passage which follows the story, Jesus calls himself the light of the world. You might anticipate that an editor would insert something spectacular like the transfiguration to depict that light. Instead, we have this story which undoubtedly was recounted in the early church. Greek scholar Bruce Metzger agrees that while Johannine authorship is doubtful, "the account has all the earmarks of historical veracity."[1]

This story demonstrates that Jesus was God and that in the midst of moral darkness, he was the light filled with grace and with truth. This story, in its own way, reveals a great deal about Jesus and the Father who sent him.

I don't doubt that this event actually took place. What is more, I think I understand why it is included here. If no one else understood him that day, if no one else saw his light, one woman did. It has always been true, I think, that the folks who have two strikes against them have a clearer understanding of who Jesus is than people who think of themselves as the home-run hitters.

In this story the woman is exposed. These religious leaders bring her sin to light and cast her into darkness. Jesus deals with the darkness of her sin, but she comes to see the light.

People from all over Israel had gathered in the capital city of Jerusalem to celebrate the most joyous of all the feasts—the Feast of Tabernacles, more commonly called the Feast of Booths. The Mosaic law required all men who lived within twenty miles of Jerusalem to go up to the city for the feast. But since it was a time of great celebration, people poured into Jerusalem from all over the country.

The Feast of Booths commemorated God's gracious dealings with his people. There was a time when the nation of Israel had lived in booths, temporary dwellings in the wilderness. They subsisted on the quail and manna that God provided day by day. But then, God brought his children into a land of milk and honey, where they enjoyed prosperous harvests and a permanent homeland.

---

1. Bruce M. Metzger, *A Textual Commentary on the Greek New Testament* (London: United Bible Societies, 1971), p. 220.

So at harvest time each year, the Jews came together in Jerusalem to give thanks to God for their blessings. As a reminder that life had not always been so pleasant, the people built booths to live in during the week of the feast. These structures were similar to the dwellings of their forefathers in the wilderness—makeshift shelters of palm fronds and willow branches with loosely thatched roofs. Jerusalem resembled a happy shantytown during the week-long festival. Temporary shacks sprang up in every available place—in the streets, in public gardens, on the flat rooftops of houses all over the city.

Now with the fields of barley and wheat harvested and stored for winter, the people of God were ready to celebrate and give thanks to God. Many came to give praise and offer sacrifices at the temple. But as often happens with religious holidays observed year after year, the Feast of Booths had become for the average Jew a week-long bash, devoid of much significance. It's the same with our great holidays, isn't it? For most Americans, Thanksgiving has become merely a day for sumptuous eating and football games. And at Christmastime, while some still remember the gift of the Christ child, most simply look for brightly wrapped presents under the tree. Just as our great occasions for worship and thanksgiving have degenerated into times for food and booze and commercialism, so the Feast of Booths represented for the majority a week of revelry, drunkenness, and debauchery. It rather resembled a modern-day Mardi Gras.

It is here that our story takes place—at the end of a week-long carnival in the city of Jerusalem. As dawn broke that day, most of the city could be found sprawled in their flimsy booths, sleeping off hangovers. There were some, however, who had come to Jerusalem to worship and they could be seen making their way to the temple. There was one particularly curious group who came to the temple that morning.

"At dawn he appeared again in the temple courts, where all the people gathered around him, and he sat down to teach them. The teachers of the law and the Pharisees brought in a woman caught in adultery" (vv. 2–3a).

What a scene! Who was this woman? How was she caught in adultery, in the very act?

There's really no indication that she was a prostitute by trade. The text merely calls her "a woman caught in adultery," not a "harlot" or a "prostitute." It's doubtful that the Pharisees had fished her out of the local red light district.

In fact, I tend to think she was just a young woman who had given up her virtue too easily. The text indicates she was guilty of adultery, so she was probably married. Perhaps her husband was out of the country on business. He may have been a merchant off closing a deal in Egypt or Syria. Transportation was slow in the first century and long trips took months. He may have been away for several weeks, with some weeks still to go. And he had left his wife at home, alone, at one of the happiest times of the year.

Perhaps she went with friends one night to a party. They sang and danced into the late hours of the evening. The mood was carefree. Laughter came easily and the wine flowed freely. There she met a man who would take away her loneliness.

He was a dark-eyed young Jew, deeply tanned from long hours spent harvesting his fields beyond the city walls. He was alone, having come to Jerusalem to celebrate the feast. As they laughed and chattered through the dance, he persuaded her to leave the party with him to look for other parties and more entertainment. For the first time in weeks she felt attractive, energetic, happy.

They wound their way gaily through the crowded streets, moving from cafe to cafe. As the parties disbanded and the streets calmed down, they found themselves near the entrance of the young man's festival booth. Of course, we can only imagine what happened, but we do know that in the early morning hours they entered the world of their own intimate affair, surrounded by a curtain of darkness.

However, as daybreak burst out over the hills of Jerusalem, there came with it sudden exposure. Passing through the cluttered streets on their way to the temple, a band of Pharisees and scribes spied the entwined couple through the loosely tied branches of the booth. They grabbed the young woman from the embrace of her lover.

Startled and confused, she clutched her garments to cover her nakedness. She instinctively reached for the arm of her young man, but he was gone. Seeing the religious robes of the Pharisees, he had bolted off down an alleyway. She begged the men for mercy and reprieve, but they dragged her from the shelter into the street.

Questions flooded her mind as she fought back hot tears of fear, humiliation, and anger. How could he leave her alone— exposed and vulnerable? He had whispered the promises of love in her ear, but in a moment he was gone, as false as his words.

Why had the religious leaders singled her out in the carnival crowd? If they wanted to clean up the immorality in the city, why hadn't they started with the well-known brothels? Or even with any one of the booths around her? Why her?

What would become of her now? How could she ever face her husband? What would she say to him?

Oh! Why had she ever given herself to someone in the first place? She felt cheapened, rejected, destroyed.

The religious leaders only aggravated her guilt. They bandied her about and called her names. They would show her—a woman of her kind deserved the punishment she would get. They pulled her, sobbing and stumbling, through the narrow streets. Anyone peering out a window at the commotion below could decipher the Pharisees' faces and find there contempt for the woman and indignation for her sin.

As they entered the temple courts, they saw a small group gathered around Jesus. He was sitting among them explaining the Scriptures, but they didn't hesitate to interrupt the lesson.

Casting the exposed adulteress into the midst of the group, they demanded, "Teacher, this woman was caught in the act of adultery. In the Law Moses commanded us to stone such women. Now what do you say?" (vv. 4–5).

These men were the moral pillars of the Jewish community, upholders of all that was good and holy. At least that is what they appeared to be. Listening to them, you might think they were distressed at the carnival atmosphere of the city at a time when the people should be worshiping. You might think they had launched a campaign to clean up the streets—beginning with this woman. At least that's the way it seemed. But things aren't always as they seem. Righteousness is not always what it appears to be.

In verse 6 we learn their real intent in seizing the woman: "They were using this question as a trap, in order to have a basis for accusing him."

What kind of trap was this? How did they design it? We can only imagine. We do know that the Jewish leaders were already plotting to have Jesus put away. In fact, at the beginning of the week they had sent their court officers to arrest him. But the temple guards returned empty-handed. They had been impressed with Jesus' teaching and found that the crowd loved him.

The Pharisees knew it would be no easy matter to take Jesus. The best way, they decided, would be to trip him up in his teaching. They were looking for the chance.

So that morning as they headed to the temple, they happened to see the illicit lovers locked in an embrace. Ordinarily, they would have looked the other way. But one of the men, a sharp theologian, saw that he could turn that act to their advantage. "Look," he said, "why don't we catch Jesus between his love for the rabble and his regard for the law? If he chooses the woman, the crowds will begin to question his teaching. If he chooses the law, he'll lose his following." The Pharisees decided to use the lovers to bait their trap for Jesus.

They were only quick enough to grab the woman—the man got away. But no matter. One sinner was all they needed for this test. One piece in the game can decide the winner. And this young woman was their pawn.

It didn't matter to the Pharisees whether this woman was stoned to death or not. The life they wanted was Jesus'. They weren't really concerned with her sin or with her. She was merely a convenience to them—"Exhibit A" in a crucial test case.

That was the mood as they dragged her before Jesus that morning. That was the reason for their question. It all appeared so righteous, so theological. But the appearance was false. Their real intentions set a vicious snare for Jesus.

Jesus knew these men. He perceived the dilemma they proposed. Even more, he saw beyond them to that woman who stood before them all in shame and humiliation. To him she was not "Exhibit A," but a hurting sinner, who had indeed violated the law, but who needed grace, forgiveness, restoration. Jesus took in the meaning of the whole scene at a glance. But then he did a strange thing. As the Pharisees hurled their questions like stones at him, Jesus stooped over and began to write on the ground with his finger.

You can imagine what the Pharisees must have thought. "Ha! We've stumped him now. He doesn't know what to say. He's just buying time."

One thing becomes clear, though, as we look on that scene. In stooping over to write in the dust, Jesus takes the eyes of the crowd off the woman, shuddering in bitter shame, and draws their attention to himself.

What was he writing? Was he just doodling or was it something more significant? We'll never really know, of course, what he wrote. Some of the ancient manuscripts added a line that does not appear in our Bibles: "and with his finger he wrote on the ground—the sins of each one of them." Hypocrite, liar, deceiver, gossip, dishonoring of parents. He would have known their sins. It's possible that's what he wrote on the ground.

His delay in answering the Pharisees only caused them to insist more loudly, "What do you say then, man? Shall we stone her?" They pressed in upon him, demanding a response.

He straightened up and said to them, 'If any one of you is without sin, let him be the first to throw a stone at her' " (v. 7b). And having said that—that one single sentence—he stooped down and wrote on the ground again.

The Pharisees had paraded themselves before the people as morally superior bastions of holiness and righteousness. Their facades had been so credible that they themselves had come to believe the mask for the truth. The Pharisees could tell you everything that was wrong about everyone else and everything that was right about themselves. That's the way it is with Pharisees, wherever you meet them—in the first century or in the twentieth century; in Jerusalem or your hometown.

We can see the seeds of Phariseeism planted in the soils of our own lives. A businessman can be incensed with the bribery that goes on in Washington, yet not think twice about cheating on his income tax. We take note of some friend who is a gossip and overlook completely the fact that we are gossiping to someone else about the gossip. The sins we keenly perceive in others may blind us to the sin in our own lives. We can be so angry at other people's sins that we are tempted to reach down and pick up stones, only to be brought up short when we hear Jesus say, "If any one of you is without sin, let him be the first to throw a stone. . . ."

That's all he had to say. No sermon. No long indictment. A single sentence. Then he went back to writing on the ground.

"At this, those who heard began to go away one at a time, the older ones first . . ." (v. 9). That's the way the writer of the story puts it, but you can't help imagining what occurred. A younger scribe may have sneered and leaned over to scoop up some stones. But a Pharisee standing next to him held his arm and nodded with eyes wide toward the temple entrance. There, toward the shaft of morning light streaming in now through the columns, one of the older, more venerated of the religious men, shuffled out, his head bowed and his eyes cast down. Had Jesus said, "Let the most respectable cast the first stone," that old man would have qualified. If he had said, "Let the most religious hurl it," that man could have been the stone-thrower. But Jesus hadn't said that. "If any one of you is without sin, let him be the first to throw a stone at her." Whatever his self-righteousness was, no matter how puffed up his opinion about himself, on that he could not qualify.

Then another white-headed leader started for the doorway, followed silently, sullenly, by a string of greying men in flowing robes. The younger man forgot the stones and rose slowly to follow the troupe of religious leaders out of the temple.

Stunned by Jesus' words and snared in their own trap, the Pharisees and scribes filed out, leaving the woman behind them. They had, in fact, forgotten she was there. Their test had backfired. They had lost another bout with the masterful young teacher.

When Jesus shone his light upon their lives, they were exposed as no better than the sinners they used their laws to condemn. The truth they claimed to uphold defeated them. Had they responded to the light Jesus offered, they would have found his grace. For Jesus loved Pharisees as much as he loved that woman. He simply spoke that word and then went back to writing on the ground. He was occupied with his writing as the Pharisees left the temple.

What was he scribbling this time? Perhaps he thoughtfully sketched the figure of a cross through the list of sins that stared up at him from the dirt—hypocrite, liar, gossip, adulteress. His thoughts may have raced forward to the days to come when he would bear each of those sins and more. While he would commit no sin, he would become as dark as sin itself in the sight of the holy God, his Father.

We do not know, of course, that he scratched the symbol of a cross on the sand, but we do know that all his life the shadow of the cross hung over him. For he came to die for that woman, those Pharisees, me, and each of you—for the whole world.

As the last of the religious leaders left the temple court, Jesus slowly straightened up and faced the woman for the first time. "Woman, where are they? Has no one condemned you?"

"No one, sir."

No doubt she was a bit bewildered by the whole thing. She had been caught in her sin. She knew she was guilty—there was no other plea. And these religious men who were so moral and upright; these accusers—suddenly they were gone. Could it be true that not one of them could cast a stone at her? They had hurled verbal stones, but could it be that before God they could not throw even a pebble? She was confused. She was frightened. What would he do with her now? She was, after all, guilty. Surely she was due some punishment for her sin.

It's strange, isn't it, the things that sin can do to us. Somehow, it has an unbalancing effect on our lives. On the one hand, we may regard our own sin too lightly, as did the Pharisees, and focus on the worst in others. At that point, we're tempted to cast stones at other sinners and disregard our own hidden deeds. On the other hand, our sin can overwhelm us so that we can see nothing else. Hounded by guilt, we look for punishment and chastisement. Inwardly we sense that all those around us have a perfect right to hurl stones and stinging abuse. We almost cry out for punishment. Sin does that to us. It unbalances us.

The only one who could have stoned the woman that morning was Jesus. He was without sin. He could have stoned her, but he did not.

" 'Woman, where are they? Has no one condemned you?' " " 'No one, sir,' she said. 'Then neither do I condemn you,' Jesus declared. 'Go now and leave your life of sin' " (vv. 10–11).

As she looked into his face, she knew for certain that she was a free woman, fully forgiven. There was not the slightest trace of condemnation in his eyes or in his voice. She stepped into the light of day feeling whole, feeling clean, feeling restored. She may not have fully understood *how* he could send her away forgiven. But that he had the power to do so, she never doubted. The only man who could have stoned her forgave her instead. Her story that had had such a sordid beginning, ended in stunning triumph—a story of God's forgiveness.

When the light of the world shines his spotlight on your soul, you have a choice in the way you'll respond. Like the religious leaders you can go on in darkness. Like roaches exposed to the light, you can flee from its brightness. Or like the woman, you may see yourself totally exposed by the light of his truth and feel as she must have felt.

Today you may feel deeply uncomfortable because of a sin you have committed. You may be embarrassed to be with friends or to face the people around you because somehow you sense that if they knew your sin, they would hurl stones of judgment and rejection at you. But look again. All your accusers have left the room. Not one of them can condemn you.

But now, like that adulteress, you may be face to face with God. You may be so overwhelmed with the burden of guilt for your sin that deep inside, you wonder if even God could forgive you. Your sins are too dark, too evil, too many, too often. Listen carefully to the words Jesus spoke to that woman in the temple long ago. Listen very carefully, because he not only speaks them to her; he speaks them to you. Whatever your sin, hear him as he says to you, "Neither do I condemn you. Go now and leave your life of sin." If you respond to him in faith and trust in this word of complete forgiveness, you can walk into the light without fear.

When the light of the world exposes our sin, we either choose the darkness or walk with him in grace and truth.

SERMON

191

Content and form relate to each other like a foot in a shoe. Some homileticians, however, have advertised a glass slipper they claim will suit Cinderella not only when she attends the ball, but also when she goes jogging and, in addition, the same slipper will fit all her sisters as well. One shoe cannot fit all. While the form is integral to the sermon, the Holy Spirit uses different shoes for different feet and different purposes.

Communicators in the early church changed forms depending on what they had to say to different audiences in particular situations. Paul taught in the synagogues like a rabbi, argued his case before Felix like a lawyer, and debated in the market-places like a philosopher. He wrote out his ideas in well-reasoned correspondence that reads like a lawyer's brief and in informal notes to good friends. John portrayed the conflicts and climax of history as we know it through apocalyptic literature filled with symbols and visions. In Acts, Luke wove theology into a travelogue, while in the Gospels he and the other biographers of Jesus spun narratives as interesting as short stories. Clearly, the Holy Spirit used many forms and was tied to none.

A preacher, therefore, should not start with form. As a case in point, during the celebration of Pentecost, Peter did not set out to preach something called a "sermon." Instead, he knew his theology could explain life to a bewildered crowd. By appealing to their sacred writings, their national heroes, and their experiences, he convinced them they had made God their enemy and, worse, had hung their only hope for salvation on a Roman execution rack. Without benefit of a course in homiletics, Peter preached one of the world's great sermons. He knew where he wanted to go and where he had to begin, and from those two fixed points, his message found its form.

Expository sermons, therefore, are not identified by the form they take, whether it is a "verse by verse" analysis of a text, a didactic explanation of a doctrine, or a key word that holds the points together. Any form that communicates the message of a passage clearly so that the listeners understand it, accept it, and know what to do about it is adequate.

COMMENTARY

194

Nancy Hardin decided the most effective way to communicate the message and theology of John 8:1–12 lay in retelling the story. She knows that we live life on the ground floor of experience not at the roof-top of abstractions. When a preacher communicates about love, grace, truth, or forgiveness only as a proposition to be explained or proved, she or he may never get down to life. A story helps an expositor conduct business where people shop for meaning. In the final analysis, a preacher's task is not to get some truth out of the Bible, but to get people into the Bible to experience its truth for themselves.

The first twelve verses of John 8 have some sand traps that must be negotiated in order to teach it; the most obvious is a textual problem. Ordinarily, the decisions an exegete makes about textual traditions in her study never get into the sermon, but in this passage the textual problem cannot be skirted. Most English translations flag it with the notation "the earliest and most reliable manuscripts do not have John 7:53–8:11" so that even the most casual reader realizes something is amiss.

Hardin faces the textual difficulty head on. When an obvious question is not acknowledged or dealt with, it resembles static on the radio. It irritates the listener and gets in the way of the message. She actually turns the difficulty to her advantage. Curiosity kills cats, but it can give life to an introduction, so she uses the problem to win attention for her narrative. Hardin also uses the question about the text as an opportunity to place her passage within the broad context of John's Gospel, something that might be more clumsy within the narrative itself. Finally, she does not trip on the technicalities of textual criticism but instead quotes an authority, Bruce Metzger, to testify on behalf of the historical veracity of the account. In a different sermon with another form, Hardin might have spent more time helping her audience understand how scholars work with ancient manuscripts. But not now.

Hardin speaks mainly to women's groups, and while this story is unfolded from the perspective of a third-person story-teller, Hardin is not neutral. Her narration reflects the empathy of a woman for a woman.

The romance of narratives comes through research into the history and customs of the past. In the telling of the story, that material must be sketched with flair and color. Hardin weaves information about the Feast of Tabernacles, why it was held, who attended, and what took place into story form rather than handle it as an entry under "Tabernacle—Feast of" in an encyclopedia. She uses analogies of our modern national holidays (Thanksgiving, Christmas) to help her audience experience the flavor of ancient Jewish holy days.

To keep the characters in a narrative from seeming as flat as paper dolls, the interpreter must approach the biblical account both with the mind and the imagination. Hardin enlarges on two scraps of information—that the woman was taken in adultery and that she alone was taken—to set the scene for the encounter with Jesus. If the central idea of the narrative hung on only those two facts, it would have lacked adequate support. But Hardin uses them to set the stage and to provide a flash of insight into the motives of the Pharisees and feelings of their victim.

In a narrative, application is usually quickly drawn and, as in a play, is often subtle and indirect. A story should carry its own message without moralizing. The fit to life comes through identification with the central characters. Hardin does not belabor her application.

The outline of the story sermon can be laid out like the plot of a play. The big idea is "When the light of the world exposes our sin we can either turn away from him in blindness or stay with him and find forgiveness in the reflection of his grace and truth." That idea is then developed in a series of scenes.

   I. We meet Jesus, the light of the world, caught in a dilemma.
      A. A young woman is caught in the act of adultery.
      B. The Pharisees use her to place Jesus in a dilemma between showing grace to a sinner and upholding the truth of the law.
  II. Jesus, the light of the world, exposes the condition of all men and women.
      A. Jesus turned the attention of the crowd from the Pharisees to himself.
      B. Jesus turned his light on the Pharisees and exposed their sin.
      C. Jesus turned his light on the sinful woman and exposed their sin.
 III. We have a choice when we are exposed by Jesus, the light of the world.
      A. We can turn away from the light and choose darkness.
      B. We can stand in the light and find forgiveness in his grace and truth.

What kind of speaking do you do?

I speak primarily to women in the context of conferences and week-end retreats around the country as well as a weekly Bible study in Denver. I also teach classes in speaking and Bible study methods for women at Denver Seminary. Sometimes I serve as an adjunct faculty member in homiletics there.

Do you think speaking to women poses any particular difficulties or challenges?

The advantage of speaking to women is that I'm able to single them out. Rather than dealing in generic illustrations that could fit male or female, I can concentrate entirely on women.

The danger is supposing all women are the same. Putting it another way, I don't think that simply because I'm a woman speaking to women I can expect them to have the same reactions to life I might have.

Do you try to analyze your audience before you speak to them?

It's critical for me to know as much about the audience as I can before an event.

What do you look for?

I look for the stages this specific group of women is in—are there singles, professional women, young marrieds, moms of pre-schoolers, moms of teenagers, working mothers, single mothers, empty-nest moms, widows, seniors? Of course, the broader the spectrum of women in one audience, the greater the challenge to meet them where they live.

Do women have many things in common as an audience?

While I don't think of all women being like me, I find, on the other hand, that women in particular respond to personal experiences and appreciate vulnerability in a way that differs from a group of men or even a mixed group. Since women are highly attuned to relationships and to their feelings about how life is going for them and those they love, they expect me to bring the Bible and experience to bear in a practical, specific way. That's a challenge I enjoy!

We've asked the other contributors this question. How much time do you put into the preparation of a sermon?

A great deal depends on whether I am teaching through a book as I might for the weekly Bible study or preparing a topical series for a retreat. I would say it probably takes me twenty hours on the average to prepare a message.

Was that true for this particular one from John 8?

Yes.

This is a difficult passage. Why did you choose it?

Frankly, I was inspired. I heard Bo Matthews preach on this passage a few years ago, and the story so grabbed me as he related it that I was compelled to study it on my own. Although my life looks nothing like the woman of the story, I strongly identified with her as "a sinner saved by grace" and I wanted to share that grace with other women.

What special problems did you encounter in working with this text?

Obviously, the textual problem posed the primary difficulty. Did John write it? If not, how did it appear in his Gospel? Is it even scriptural?

Then, having researched that issue, I faced the next problem of how much explanation to include in this message. In many ways, this was the more difficult question for me. I meet many women who would not be satisfied with glossing over the problem, but most people are not interested in the complexities of textual criticism. I tried to take the textual problem seriously without treating it extensively.

One other problem I found in dealing with the text was how to place this story in a wider context of the Book of John. Here I had to look for implications of the story since there are no explicit words or statements which tie it into what goes before or what follows.

Why did you decide to handle this as a third-person narrative?

To be honest, I didn't sit down and contemplate what form to use for the story. The third-person narrative simply flowed from it for me.

You didn't use any formal illustrations. Do you feel illustrations are important?

The narrative itself is like an extended illustration. In imagining what may have taken place, I already had a lot of concrete, specific material that serves the function of structured illustrations in other messages. In other kinds of talks, when I'm explaining or proving or applying a concept, I use all kinds of illustrations. But in this story there aren't a lot of abstractions or principles which need to be made concrete.

INTERVIEW

Chapter 10

How to Stand Perfect in the Sight of God
Romans 4:5

Larry Moyer

Larry Moyer began his ministry of evangelism in 1973 when he founded EvanTell, an evangelistic organization based in Dallas, Texas. He has traveled throughout the country speaking to adults and young people in churches, areawide crusades, camps, Bible conferences, and conferences on evangelism. He has also held crusades outside the United States.

Sermon

The story is told of an immigrant who enlisted in the United States Army during World War II. Being a foreigner, he had great difficulty with the English language. One day as the troop prepared for inspection, the men realized that unless they gave this soldier some help, he would flunk, simply due to his difficulty with English. So one of the men said to him, "Now look. In a few days, the general is going to come around, and unless you are extremely careful, you could fail inspection simply due to your problems with the language. Let me tell you the questions he'll probably ask and the answers you need to be prepared to give.

"The first question he'll undoubtedly ask is, 'How long have you been in the army?' When he asks that, simply answer, 'Two years.' The second question he will undoubtedly ask is, 'How old are you?' When he asks that, answer, 'Twenty-two.' The third question he will undoubtedly ask is, 'Have you been receiving good food and good treatment?' When he asks that, tell him, 'Both.' Two, Twenty-two, and Both. As long as you can remember those three answers you should have no difficulty. But whatever you do, don't forget: Two, Twenty-two, and Both."

The day of the inspection came and, sure enough, the general did ask three questions. The only problem was, he did not ask them in the order in which the soldier was prepared to answer them. Instead, he said, "I'd like to ask you a few questions. First, how old are you?" The soldier answered, "Two years." The general looked at him and said, "Well, how long have you been in the army?" and the soldier answered, "Twenty-two years." The general looked at him and said, "What do you take me for—an idiot or a fool?" And the soldier answered, "Both."

I am certain all of us are delighted that we did not stand in the shoes of that poor soldier when it came to the day of inspection. Yet each of us is keenly aware that we are going to participate in a far greater inspection, because we are going to stand before the Architect of the universe, the God of everything living and everything not living, and there give account of ourselves. Hebrews 9:27 says that "man is destined to die once, and after that to face judgment."

It has been my experience that when you mention a day of judgment to people, their thoughts are many and varied. Some look forward to it, and others seem to fear it. Some feel hopeful, while others feel hopeless. Some think they stand a chance, and others wonder if they have any chance at all. But for the most part, when you mention the day of judgment to people, their thoughts are not pleasant. They dread the idea of standing before God, knowing their life will be as an open book before him. For that reason, most people get about as excited about the day of judgment as they get about their dentist appointments.

Some time ago, a teenager called the dentist's office and told the secretary, "I need to make an appointment." The secretary answered, "The dentist is out of town. Can you call back again?" The teenager responded, "I'd be delighted to. When will he be out of town again?"

That is the way most feel about the day of judgment. It is not something they are particularly looking forward to. Yet, in one verse of Scripture God has an encouraging word to give every person here. Because in that one verse, he tells you how you can stand as perfect before him as his own Son stands—not five years from now or fifty years from now, but now, right now, you can stand as perfect before God as his own Son stands. That verse is Romans 4:5. To understand what God is saying in this verse and why he is saying it, you have to understand that there are three questions God is *not* asking you—the very questions most people are convinced he *is* asking.

The first question that Romans 4:5 makes clear that God is not asking is, "How many good works have you done?" Most are of the opinion that being accepted by God is based on what you do. Therefore, the more you increase your good works down here, the more you increase your chances up there. Ask someone, "Do you think you're going to heaven?" and he'll likely reply, "I'm working toward it." But the first question that Romans 4:5 makes clear that God is not asking is, "How many good works have you done?" If you will notice, the first phrase says, "to the man who does not work. . . ." God does not accept anyone on the basis of how many good works he or she has performed.

God even tells you why he cannot accept you on that basis. Glance back to verse 4. "Now when a man works, his wages are not credited to him as a gift, but as an obligation." If God were to accept you on the basis of your good works, all he would be doing is paying a debt, giving you something he owes you. What the Bible is saying is that God will not be in debt to any individual. God is not about to owe you anything. Therefore, he is not asking, "How many good works have you done?"

Let's suppose that you own the most spacious mansion in the state of Texas. It is a three-story house with a two-story basement. It has carpet one-inch thick throughout the whole house. It has the latest in modern furniture. It has a fireplace and a chandelier in every room. It has a bowling alley, a tennis court, and a swimming pool all in the basement! It has trees in the front yard whose limbs look like they would touch heaven. It has an acre of grass on all sides of the house.

Let's suppose that I come to you and ask, "May I come and live with you?" You say, "Sure, Larry. I'd be glad to have you. All I ask is that you do these ten things," and you give me a list of ten things that includes everything from loving my wife—which

I do—to loving my mother-in-law—which I'm *trying* to do. Nevertheless, I do those ten things. At the end of the time, you let me into your house. All you'd be doing is paying a debt, giving me something you owe me. What the Bible is saying is, if God were to accept you on the basis of your good works, all he would be doing is paying a debt, giving you something he owes you. What the Scriptures are saying is that God will not be in debt to any man. God is not about to owe you anything.

So the first question that Romans 4:5 makes clear God is not asking is, "How many good works have you done?"

Romans 4:5 makes clear that there is a second question God is not asking you. Not only is he not asking how many good works you have performed; the second question he is not asking is, "How well have you behaved?" If you asked some people, "Do you think you're going to heaven?" one of the first things they'll say is, "I think I stand a better chance than a lot of people!" If you ask, "Why do you say that?" they reply, "Because I've never been in jail, I don't stick my nose in other people's business, and I try to do what is right." The only problem with that is that God is not asking, "How well have you behaved?" If you will notice, the middle of verse 5 says, "but trusts God who justifies the wicked. . . ." It's a matter of believing, not a matter of behaving—and the two are as different as day is from night.

Notice again, God tells you why he cannot accept you on the basis of your behavior. No matter how well you behave, you are still "ungodly." Look again at the middle of verse 5. We think we know what "ungodly" means, but then again we're not sure. For years I heard the word *epistle* but I could not figure out for the life of me what an epistle was. Finally, I concluded that an epistle was probably the wife of an apostle. I mean, that made a lot of sense to me. Here's Mr. Apostle and here's his wife Mrs. Epistle. We have that same kind of problem with the word *ungodly*. But all that word *ungodly* means is that there have been times when you've been irreverent and you have not lived as righteously as God says you ought to live.

You're probably thinking, "Now, Larry, hold everything just a minute. I am not convinced that's true." The reason you're not convinced that's true is that when you consider how ungodly you've been, you compare yourself with the worst criminal you've ever heard of, and you come out looking like an angel. But when God considers how ungodly you've been, he compares you to the most perfect individual who ever lived, his Son Jesus Christ. Now, his Son never told a lie; you already have a pocketful of those. His Son never had one wrong thought; you average a minimum of two a day. His Son never even hated his enemies; you have times when you can't stand the person you're married to! It doesn't matter how you slice it. He knows everything you've done. He knows every word you've spoken. He knows every thought you've had. All he can say about you is, "Ungodly."

If you go back in the pages of history, you'll find there was once a wicked emperor named Dionysius. One day, he discovered that near to where he lived was a cave shaped in the form of an inverted funnel with an opening right at the earth's surface. Dionysius decided to use that cave as a workshop for his slaves. He would put all the slaves into the cave and then go up and put his ear to the top of it. Inside were the slaves uttering all kinds of harsh and cruel things about him. The next day they were brought before him to hear everything they had said repeated to them. For many of them, it cost them severe torture or their lives.

Obviously, God is a good King, not a wicked one. At the same time, he knows every thought you've had. He knows every word you've spoken. He knows everything you've done, and all he can say about you is, "Wicked." Even your best does not impress him; therefore, he is not asking, "How well have you behaved?"

You say, "Then, Larry, if it's a matter of believing and not behaving, what does 'believe' mean?" Before we examine that word, there's one other word we have to examine. That is the word *justifies*. Notice that the middle of verse 5 says, "but trusts God who justifies the wicked...." Now all that word *justifies* means is to declare you the opposite of what you are right now. In other words, you have told a pocketful of lies; God would like to declare you a person who has never told one. You have had one wrong thought after another; God would like to declare you a person who has never had a wrong thought. You've had times when you hated your best friend; God would like to declare you a person who has never known hate.

You ask, "How can he do that?" There is only one way he can. Sin cannot be passed over. Sin must be punished, and the punishment for sin is death. But the reason God can declare you righteous is that somebody else, his Son, has taken that punishment and died in your place.

Some of us remember reading back in 1974 about the new twenty-four-story bank building in São Paulo, Brazil, that burned to the ground. Several air conditioners on the twelfth floor had not been wired properly. There were 600 employees in the building at the time; 188 of them died. One-third died when they either jumped or fell to their death. One-fourth died when they went to the top floor to escape the flames and, instead, were trapped by them. The reason even more people did not die was an elevator operator. She had been told to get out of that building and forget about the elevator, but she refused to do so. Instead, she kept going up and down the building, bringing as many as twenty-five people to safety every time. She went up to get a fourth load, and when the elevator hit the twentieth floor, the power shut off. The next day, they found her charred body lying by the door of the elevator. She saved people by dying for them. She died in their place.

What the Bible is saying is, Christ saved you by dying for you. He died in your place and arose again the third day. Therefore, the reason God can declare you righteous is because somebody else, his Son, has taken the punishment. All you have to do is believe.

Now, quite honestly, we use that word *believe* for everything and anything under the sun. For example, a husband says to his wife, "Believe me, I will be in from golfing by three o'clock." What she doesn't realize is that he means three o'clock A.M., not P.M. A wife says to her husband, "Believe me, the dress was on sale." Then she tells him what the sale price was! A child says to his parents, "Believe me, I did my homework." But, apparently after he did it, he made an airplane out of it and somebody hijacked it.

We use that word *believe* for everything and anything under the sun, but the word *believe* in the Bible means two things. It means "to accept something as being true," and then it means "to trust." For example, of all the people who ever walked across Niagara Falls on a tightrope, the most spectacular had to be the Great Blondin. The first time he crossed was on June 30, 1859. The next year, he walked across on stilts, walked across with his hands and feet chained, and even carried a stove across on which he cooked an omelet at the halfway point. Now that really fascinates me. I can't cook an omelet when I'm *not* on a tightrope, and he did it on a tightrope. His most spectacular feat of all was carrying his manager on his back across the tightrope.

I've been told that one time the Great Blondin walked up to somebody who had seen him do all these things and asked him, "Would you like me to take you across?" The man "split"! All he left behind was a cloud of dust. Frankly, he may have believed the Great Blondin could do it, but he did not trust him to do it. When the Bible uses the word *believe,* it means to accept as true that God the Father will declare you righteous because his Son took your punishment and trust his Son as your only way to heaven—not trusting yourself and what you've done to get yourself there, but trusting Christ and what he did. But it's a matter of believing; it is not a matter of behaving. Therefore, God is not asking, "How well have you behaved?"

If you will notice, Romans 4:5 makes it clear that there is a third question God is not asking you. Not only is he not asking, "How many good works have you done?" Not only is he not asking, "How well have you behaved?" the third question he is not asking is, "How long will you last?

Some time ago I was talking with a businessman in Del Rio, Texas. He admitted to me that he was not a Christian, so I asked him, "Well, do you understand the gospel?" He said, "Yes, I do. Christ died for me and Christ arose. If I put my trust in him, he will save me." So, I said to him, "Then why don't you do that?" His answer was, "Because I don't know how long I could last."

My response was, "The interesting thing is, that is one question God is not asking you." Notice, the end of verse 5 says, "his faith is credited as righteousness." That word *credited* means "to reckon or credit something to your account."

Let's suppose there's a big sheet of paper with a line right down the middle. One side represents your sins. The other side represents Christ's righteousness. All the Bible is saying is that the moment you put your trust in Christ, God takes his Son's righteousness and puts it on your account.

Years ago there was a well-known preacher by the name of Harry Ironside. One time he was visiting a sheep ranch in Texas where he saw one of the most peculiar animals he'd ever seen. It looked like it had two heads instead of one, four front feet instead of two, and four back feet as well. Then the rancher explained what had happened. He said, "We had a sheep bear a lamb, and the lamb died. Then we had another sheep bear a lamb, and the mother died. We needed a mother for that lamb. The other mother would not accept it. She knew it was not her own. So, we took the skin of her dead lamb, and we draped it over the living lamb. As soon as we put it in the pen, she walked over to it and seemed to say, 'That's mine.' " What the Bible is saying is, the moment you put your trust in Christ, God takes his Son's righteousness and clothes you with it. Therefore, when God looks at you, he does not see your sins; he sees only the righteousness of his Son Jesus Christ.

Therefore, it does not matter if you live five years or fifty years; you do good, pretty good, or very good; you will never be any more righteous before God than you are the day that you trust Christ.

Now, this is not to say you ought not to live a good life, you ought not to do good things. The Bible has much to say about a good life and good works as the distinguishing marks of a believer. But they cannot increase your righteousness before God. You are never any more righteous before God than you are the day that you trust Christ and God takes his Son's righteousness and clothes you with it. Therefore, he is not asking, "How long will you last?"

I know of a man who was once approached with the question, "When you stand before the Lord, what do you think is the first question he's going to ask you?" And the man responded, "I don't think he'll ask a thing! I think he'll just look at me and say, 'He's mine.'" The truth of the matter is, when God looks upon you right now, he either sees your sin because you've never trusted Christ, or he sees his Son's righteousness because you have. If he sees his Son's righteousness, all he will say is, "he belongs to me." Therefore, he is not asking, "How long will you last?"

How to stand perfect in the sight of God? The answer is simple: Trust Jesus Christ as your only way to heaven. God is not asking, "How many good works have you done?" It is to the man who does not work. God is not asking, "How well have you behaved?" It's a matter of believing, not behaving. God is not asking, "How long will you last?" The moment you trust Christ, he clothes you with his Son's righteousness, and you stand perfect in his sight.

How to stand perfect in the sight of God? The answer is so simple that there are millions who are missing it: trust Jesus Christ. We by nature want to work to get it, behave to deserve it, and try in order to keep it. So, when God wants to do something simply out of his own goodness, it's extremely difficult for us to receive it.

Some time ago, I flew to Indiana for some meetings. When I got off the plane, the pastor who greeted me said, "There is a lady driving a hundred miles to see you tomorrow morning. She says she just has to talk to you. If you remember, the first time you were at our church, you spent hours trying to get this woman to see the simple plan of salvation." I clearly remembered the woman. I had spent whole afternoons trying to get her to see it.

She came the next morning. When she walked up to me after the service, she said, "I just had to come to tell you that I'm saved." I looked at her and said, "I don't know who is the most excited—you, the Lord, the angels, or me—but I do know that I'm glad to hear that. Now tell me a little bit about it."

She said, "Well, it happened six months after you and I talked." She continued to explain what she meant by that. Then I said to her, "Well, look, just for my own benefit in helping others to understand the gospel, is there anything I may have said that finally helped you to see it?" She said, "Yes, in fact, there was. You kept saying over, and over, and over, and over, and over, 'It's too simple. That's why you can't get it. It's too simple. If God said to you, 'To get to heaven, you've got to go to church three Sundays, you have to be baptized four times, you have to take five sacraments, and you have to live a good life for six years,' you would go to church three Sundays, you would be baptized four times, you would take five sacraments, and you would live a good life for six years. But when God says, 'Will you trust Christ and be declared righteous in the sight of God?' that is so simple you can't get it.' "

She said, "Six months later, it dawned on me what you meant. I trusted Christ, and I know I'm saved."

Frankly, you don't have to wait six months. You can trust Jesus Christ this moment and be declared perfect in the sight of God. For the moment you do, he makes you a promise, and he puts it in no more than twenty words: "However, to the man who does not work but trusts God who justifies the wicked, his faith is credited as righteousness."

Expository sermons and evangelistic preaching sometimes make a difficult marriage. The passages that ask the right questions appear to give the wrong answers. For example, "What must I do to inherit eternal life?" asked by a Jewish theologian comes up with the answer "Keep the law with regard to God and neighbor" (Luke 10:25–28). The preacher must spend quite a bit of time explaining why Jesus' answer was an impossible requirement to fulfill and, after that, introduce the gospel which isn't clearly given in the passage. Other passages which explain the gospel often do so in contexts that raise questions modern audiences don't care much about or are separated by paragraphs from where the biblical writer brings up the question.

Larry Moyer provides an evangelistic sermon from Romans 4:5 that handles both Bible thought and the audience with integrity. Three factors in this sermon make it worth studying. First, the sermon is fashioned for non-Christians. Its inductive development is ideal for an audience indifferent or antagonistic to a direct presentation of the gospel. The evangelist starts with the assumptions of the listener before he gets to the message of God. After discussing questions God is not asking, Moyer then presents what God is asking and God's answer.

The sermon, therefore, presupposes that thoughtful unbelievers have questions that must be surfaced before they will trust Jesus Christ. Not only does the outline develop around three key questions non-Christians have but in the development of the sermon Moyer poses at least twenty-six other questions.

The sermon also relates to non-Christians by its use of humor. Research shows that nonchurched people feel that churches are gloomy and preachers constantly talk about money and death. Although Moyer talks candidly about the day of judgment, he gets to that topic with humor; and having introduced it, he uses humor again before assuring us that God offers an encouraging word about that dreaded day. An evangelist does not dress in sackcloth and carry a sandwich board warning of doom. He wants to get people to interact with him. Humor helps a listener to accept ideas that otherwise may be hard to hear.

A second factor worth noting about this message: it is clear. Obscurity builds a wall between a speaker and the audience. An evangelist sins against his hearers when he fails to tell them in terms they can understand what God's Good News is. Jargon and unclear thought destroy life and hope and make God sound as boring as a test pattern on television. Moyer states his three questions at the beginning and the end and in the middle of each major point. His transitions before his second and third points and before his conclusion review what has been said and anticipate what follows. The sermon, although inductive, flows clearly.

Moyer's clarity is also enhanced by his generous use of illustrations. The sermon is not an abstract discussion of soteriology and *sola fides,* but the presentation of the gospel in easily understood pictures. Medieval scholars argued that universals have objective reality in the mind of God, but in the minds of ordinary men and women they are as exciting as a yawn unless captured in an illustration. Examples make generalities understandable and believable. In this sermon illustrations serve several functions: they explain, prove and apply the ideas, raise and answer objections, and infuse warmth and interest into the message.

Moyer also touches curiosity. It is the thrust of his introduction. "To understand what God is saying in this verse (Rom. 4:5) and why he is saying it, you have to understand that there are three questions God is *not* asking you—the very questions most people are convinced he *is* asking."

    I. God is *not* asking "How many good works have you done?"
       A. Romans 4:5 says "to the man who does not work. . . ."
       B. Human experience shows God is not asking how many good works you have done.
    II. God is *not* asking "How well have you behaved?"
       A. Romans 4:5 says "but trusts God who justifies the wicked. . . ." God calls for *belief,* not good behavior.
    III. God is *not* asking "How long will you last?"
       A. Romans 4:5 says "his faith is *credited* as righteousness" which shows when one believes he belongs to God.

The idea of the sermon also emerges clearly: To stand perfect in the sight of God on the day of judgment, trust Jesus Christ and nothing else.

A third important factor about this sermon: it is essentially biblical. Its content is derived from a single sentence of Scripture. While the major questions do not come from the text or even the context, the answers do come both by direct statement and necessary implication from the verse.

Although expository sermons usually draw both their ideas and development from the passage, they cannot always do so. Sometimes for the sake of listeners, the preacher approaches a text at an angle different from the biblical writer. Moyer uses the context of Romans 4:5 only once to help prove a point, but he does not appeal to the context in any other way. Yet, the ultimate test of exposition must be: "Does the content of the sermon come from the text or is it imposed on the text?" While Moyer's questions were not Paul's questions as he wrote Romans 4, Moyer's answers which form the bulk of the sermon do reflect the apostle's answers.

COMMENTARY

How long does it usually take you to prepare a message?

A minimum of twenty hours.

How long did it take you to prepare the message you submitted?

Roughly about twenty hours.

How long are your sermons normally?

Thirty minutes. I try to keep evangelistic messages to a maximum of thirty minutes. They should be short.

What passages do you think make effective evangelistic presentations?

John 3:16, John 5:24, Isaiah 53:6, Romans 3:10–18, Luke 19:1–10, Romans 5:6–8, Ephesians 2:1–10, John 3:1–15, and Luke 18:9–14 are very effective. In developing these passages, however, the art of evangelistic preaching is not only knowing what to put in, but knowing what to leave out. In an evangelistic sermon you can't go as deeply into the text as you might with an audience of believers. You have to pull out what is significant and of interest to an unchurched audience. Evangelists have been accused of ignoring the text. We've got to deal with the text, but we can't deal with it as thoroughly.

You use illustrations well. How do you come up with them?

There are two keys to getting illustrations: (1) You never go around without 3×5 cards in your pocket. This develops the drive to look for them. (2) You have to set a goal for yourself. My personal goal is ten a week. I never go under it, often I go over it. I get a minimum of 520 a year. You've got to stay committed.

What sources do you find most profitable?

My main source comes from reading. I read everything I can get my hands on. I read at least two books a month. I find *Time* magazine useful, especially for an evangelist because it tells life the way non-Christians see it. *Reader's Digest* is also helpful.

What was the greatest challenge for you in approaching the biblical text in this sermon?

Making it interesting to an unsaved person. I felt those three questions (How many good works have you done? How well have you behaved? How long will you last?) would appeal to some unconverted.

Do you often preach from a single verse?

The smaller the unit of thought the better for non-Christians. I preach many one-verse sermons, but that's not my only method. Sometimes the passage dictates that you must use several verses to get the entire idea across.

Comment on your use of humor. Do you use it often?

I don't think I've ever preached a nonhumorous evangelistic sermon. Once I step up to the pulpit I have thirty seconds to get attention (at least that is the pressure I put upon myself). Humor helps that. Humor shows that the evangelist knows how to laugh. You must use humor for communication's sake, not for humor's sake. In other words, you don't use a series of jokes and tack the gospel on at the end.

What other elements do you put into an evangelistic sermon?

Illustrations. On the average, I use ten illustrations per message. Enthusiasm! You have to be enthusiastic. You won't sell someone something you're not sold on yourself. Repetition. An evangelistic message is more repetitious than a normal message, because you are usually talking to men and women not accustomed to sitting and listening to sermons. The main idea must be stated and restated and then stated again. Simple organization. Although you're dealing with profound thoughts, the audience must be able to follow you. The best evangelistic messages are the simplest messages. Authority. Non-Christians are un-impressed with phrases like "Paul said it." So I stick to saying "God or the Bible said it." This gives the message authority. An evangelistic sermon has a clear and simple purpose—to inform and to invite. It has to be life-revealing. You not only exegete the Bible; you exegete the congregation. It has to be direct. At times you stop saying "we" and start saying "you." "You have to trust Christ." "You are here tonight, and you are lost."

If you had one comment to give to a young preacher, what would it be?

Listen and learn from preachers you respect. Old preachers have more to teach than old sermons. Charles Spurgeon's approach to sermon making has helped me more than his sermons.

INTERVIEW

219

Chapter 11

When Life Deals You a Lemon, Make a Lemonade
James

Michael Cocoris

Michael Cocoris is senior pastor of the Church of the
Open Door in Glendora, California. He is author of
*Seventy Years on Hope Street: A History of the Church
of the Open Door, 1915 –1985* and *Evangelism: A
Biblical Approach.* Previously, he served as an
evangelist holding campaigns throughout the United
States and Canada.

In the summer, my family and I moved from Dallas, Texas, to Los Angeles, California, where I was to assume the pastorate of the Church of the Open Door. My wife capitalized on the opportunity to get me to buy a piece or two of furniture. We really did want to replace the end tables in the living room. So, I said, "Okay." We decided that instead of buying them in Texas and having to pay to have them shipped to California, we would wait until we got to Los Angeles to make the purchase.

When we arrived, my wife started looking. She shopped at about six stores, and then found just what she wanted. That particular furniture store was a member of a national chain and the furniture was on sale. She loved the pieces and I liked the price, so we bought them. When we paid for the three-piece set, we were told that it would take four to six weeks for delivery. That was no problem. As a matter of fact, it was just in time for a meeting at our home with a group from the church.

Six weeks later—no furniture. We called. They said that it was a popular sale and they had been flooded with orders, but it would be along shortly.

Eight weeks later—no furniture. More explanations. Then one piece came.

Six weeks after that—a second piece came.

Six more weeks—more excuses.

What was to take six weeks was now six months. The whole thing was a hassle. Every time someone came to our home, we had to explain why the lamp was on the floor instead of on an end table. Every time I went through the living room, I thought, "When will they deliver that last end table?" At that point, I felt as if I had been dealt a lemon.

I'm sure that at some point in your life you have felt the same way. Life has a way of dealing us deuces instead of aces. Your lemon might not have been as long; it might have been a brief irritation like a fender-bender or a traffic jam, or, "I'm sorry, sir, we're out of that at the moment," or your ordeal may have been more serious like losing your boyfriend or your job or your money or your wife. But whether you are five, fifteen, or seventy-five, you've learned that life has lemons.

Now, how do you handle lemons? The answer to that question is what the Book of James is all about. To use his word, the subject of James is "trials." In the introduction, he informs us that trials come from God and lead to life (1:2–12), that is, trials are for our training. James then immediately discusses temptation as if to say with every trial there is a temptation, particularly to blame God. He reminds us that temptation comes from us and leads to death (1:13–18).

He draws a conclusion and states it in 1:19. This forms an outline of what follows. Since God allows trials to come into our lives to mature us, and since there is a danger that we might sin and miss the crown of life and make a mess, we must make sure we respond properly. If we follow this formula, we will get the most, the maximum maturity from our troubles.

When life deals you a lemon, make a lemonade. Here's the recipe for the best lemonade you've ever tasted.

First, *be quick to listen*. But to whom and when? There are several possible answers. James could be saying to be quick to listen to others generally. That, of course, is true and needs to be done. So much of our conversation is centered on our frustrations and our interests that we are deaf to what others are saying to us. Once a little boy at supper suddenly shouted in a loud voice, "Pass the potatoes!" His mother indignantly insisted that he go to his room for behaving so rudely. Later that evening his father disclosed that he had bought a new cassette tape recorder and had secretly taped the family chatter at supper time. As everyone listened eagerly, they heard loud laughter and excited talking. Then they detected a boyish voice saying, "May I please have some potatoes?" A little later the same voice said the same thing. The chatter continued and then, after several repeated requests, the voice shouted, "Pass the potatoes!" We definitely need to listen to each other.

But James is not exactly talking about being swift to hear others generally. The context of James 1:19 indicates that he is talking about being swift to hear when you are in the midst of a trial.

When trouble elbows its way into our lives, we are slow to hear anyone but ourselves. When our plans are interrupted, we erupt. When we are inconvenienced, we are incensed. Then, when anyone tries to tell us anything, we are anything but swift to hear.

James goes on to explain that hearing here is hearing God's Word (1:21). He then quickly adds that hearing God's Word means heeding God's Word (1:22–25).

The Bible is God's recipe book for making lemonade out of lemons, but obviously you have to do what it says or you'll not have lemonade. You could have the most expensive and extensive recipe book in your home. It could tell you how to make Chicken Normandie and Trout Almondine, Crab Bisque; you could have all the ingredients in the refrigerator, yet if you just read the book and did not do what it said, you would not enjoy those fine dishes. You could read and get enlightened. You could understand how to make it. You could even read and get excited, but until you have followed the directions, you have not enjoyed the food. You would also have to follow the directions exactly and entirely to get the maximum results. Some just read the book. Some start following a recipe and then stop. Some finish, but don't follow the recipe exactly. For guaranteed results, one must follow the instructions completely.

Then, all of a sudden, James discusses pure religion which he identifies as visiting the fatherless and widows (1:26–27). In other words, heeding the Word means helping people. When the lawyer asked Jesus, "What is the greatest commandment?" Jesus responded, "Love God," and the second is like it, "Love your neighbor." If you are not involved in the lives of people and investing time in ministering to them, you are simply not where God wants you to be. Furthermore, you are not handling your own problems and pressures the way God desires. We use personal problems as excuses for not visiting people to help them. James teaches that when you are in a trial, that is when you should visit people.

So, when you have a problem, be swift to hear God's Word, heed God's Word, and help God's people.

James next discusses the case of the near-sighted usher (2:1–13). He is telling us that prejudice will keep us from ministry. His readers were sharing with the rich and shunning the poor. James says that sharing with the rich is okay, but shunning the poor is not (2:8–9).

We gravitate toward those that are like us in class, age, and education. We do not naturally relate to those of a different economic or educational level, so we don't. If I understand James, he is saying to work at it, especially when you have trials. To allow biases to keep you from being involved with people is to rob them of your ministry to them and to rob you of their ministry to you.

It is no accident that the next paragraph in the Book of James deals with the concept that "faith without works is dead" (2:14–26). James is saying, "Go to work; get busy."

The sum of James 1:21–2:26, then, is to be quick to listen, that is, hear and heed God's Word and help God's people. When hurting, help others. In battle, there are always those brave ones who, even though wounded, manage to rescue others. We call them heroes. All of us have hurts. Some of us use them to excuse ourselves. Some help others in spite of their hurts.

The second thing James says is to *be slow to speak*. He discusses this exhortation in detail in chapter 3. In 3:1–12, he tells us that the tongue can do great good and great harm, and it can be inconsistent. So, be slow to speak. In 3:13–18, he talks about true godly wisdom and concludes that even if you have wisdom from heaven, show it first in your actions. In short, be slow to speak.

When I was in seminary, several men from another seminary and I formed an evangelistic association. Five of us were charter members. Most of these men were ahead of me in age and experience; I was the junior member of the team. We divided the United States into eight areas and made plans for putting a regional evangelist in each area. We printed brochures, started a mailing list, and even raised some funds. A few of these men graduated from the seminaries they were attending before I did. They entered evangelism, still committed to the idea of eight regional evangelists. Then I graduated and commenced to travel.

SERMON

227

When we met for our next meeting, they asked me how it was going. Actually, it was going very well. Some of them were having difficulties, though. As we talked, it dawned on me what they were doing. They were talking a better game than they played. I remember saying, "Beware! Don't give people promises; give them performance." These young evangelists were promising people the country and not performing in their church. That is something of what James is saying. Give me performance, not promises. Don't tell me, show me.

James 3 should be seen in light of the subject of the whole book which is trials. He is not just saying to be slow to speak normally; he is saying to be slow to speak during trials. If you are talking, you are not listening. If you are not listening, you are not learning. If you are not learning, you are not growing. If you are not growing, you are being overcome instead of being an overcomer. So, to put it plainly, shut up and listen.

The third command in James 1:19 is to *be slow to become angry*. He discusses this command in detail in 4:1–5:12. He does not use the word *wrath* or *anger* directly, but he does talk about a wrong attitude and leaving God out. "You do not have because you do not ask" (4:2) sums it up. That is, you didn't go to God.

The consequences are: war (4:1–10); judging (4:11–12); planning without considering God (4:13–17); and the poor handling of unjust treatment (5:1–12). But underneath all of this is anger at other believers, at unbelievers, and at God. The final result is physical illness (5:13–18).

As a minister, I am amazed at how often when I counsel with people that we start with a conflict and physical ailments and end up talking about anger. As I entered the auditorium to speak at a Bible conference, I saw a lady at the door whom I had met before. I simply asked, "How are you?" It was only a greeting, not an invitation for a medical report, but she said, "Not too well." I asked her what seemed to be the problem and she said, "Headaches and pain in my neck." I then inquired, "Were you in an accident?" She said, "No, but I've been to a doctor and he says there's nothing wrong with my neck." To edit the story: she, her husband, and I had a long talk. It became immediately apparent that she was having conflicts with her husband and she was angry—very angry. When she dealt with the anger and her relationship to her husband, her headaches disappeared.

To sum up the Book of James, the way to make a lemonade out of a lemon is to be quick to listen, slow to speak, and slow to become angry. These three imperatives deal with actions, words, and attitudes. When in a trial, some Christians make sure that their actions are right, but their words and attitudes aren't. As they grow, they discover that there are things they shouldn't say as well as things they shouldn't do. But underneath, their attitude is still not what it ought to be. Until all three of these areas are what God intends, there will not be the spiritual growth God wants. In other words, to get the maximum maturity out of a trial, make sure your actions, words, and attitudes are biblical.

I confess that I have not always followed the recipe, but I am learning, and a few times I have managed to follow the instructions. For example, take the case of the undelivered, but paid-for furniture. The first thing I did was occupy myself with ministry. Many times I wanted to go see the manager, but when I had to choose between that and helping someone else, I chose the latter, even on my day off. Second, I said nothing. Oh, my wife and I discussed it, she called and asked questions, but I said little else beyond that. Third, I did not get angry. To be more exact, when I felt the anger coming on, I quickly controlled it and contained it. Then I wrote a letter. Not to the salesman, not to the local manager, but to the national president on the East Coast. It read as follows:

Dear _____:

I am writing to inquire about the tree you are growing for me. How is it doing? Would you say it has a normal growth rate? When do you anticipate it reaching maturity so that it can be used? I trust that it is being watered, fertilized and cared for properly.

Let me explain. Last summer, my wife and I moved to southern California. We needed tables for our living room. After visiting many stores, my wife found a set at _____ in Pasadena that she just fell in love with. In August, we placed an order. We were told it would take four to six weeks for delivery. Several months later, the first of three pieces arrived. Then, after another month or so, the second piece arrived. The third piece has never arrived. It is now April.

We have tried to be patient and kind. On several occasions we have called and have been told repeatedly, simply that it is not in yet. We are certain you must be growing the tree for our last piece of furniture, and we're just curious how its growth is coming.

In the meantime, I think you should know that because of my position, many people visit my home. Of course, when they see a lamp sitting on the floor, we have to explain. So, dozens of times we have told the people about your tree-growing project. Now, I realize it takes a long time to grow a tree, but at least knowing when you think it might be ready would give us some kind of hope. So, could you tell us, sir, when our tree will be ready for its service?

Sincerely,
Mike Cocoris

The results were: (1) I did not get an ulcer; (2) I learned a little patience; (3) I taught my kids how to handle problems, namely, don't get upset; be patient and go to the president; (4) the furniture was delivered within seven days.

SERMON
■■■■■■■■■

230

Commentary

In 1551, Robert Estienne, a French printer, divided his Greek
New Testament into chapters and verses. This arrangement
entered the system of English translations through the popular
Geneva Bible in 1560 and culminated in the King James Bible
of 1611, the most dominant translation of all time.

As a device for quick reference and easy identification of
passages, the versification of Scripture has had undeniable value,
but we have purchased convenience at a high price. People do
not approach the Bible with the same consideration they give
to a paperback novel; instead, they treat it like a string of holy
sayings, any one of which can be singled out and made to
sound like the final word from God. As they handle the Scriptures in the pulpit, preachers take a worm's eye view of a
passage and seldom catch a bird's eye perspective of a complete section or an entire book of Scripture.

Although serious Christians must master the details of the
Word of God, individual verses of Scripture always stand in
relation to their larger units of thought. Only when we grasp
the terrain of a garden can we appreciate the placing of an
individual spruce or a particular rosebush. If we focus only on

a particular sentence, we may miss the panorama of an author's thought. On the other hand, if we grasp a sense of the whole, we will better understand the parts.

In this sermon, Michael Cocoris handles the letter from James in a single sermon. This is the concluding message of a lengthy series expounding the epistle. An overview of James poses particular challenges in that the epistle does not have a clear, well-developed argument like Romans or Hebrews. Cocoris sees James 1:19 an as umbrella which covers the broad topical development of James' thought, and he uses that text to outline his sermon on how to handle trials. Even though he gives his congregation an overview of the letter, his purpose in preaching the sermon relates to people's lives. Cocoris desires to motivate Christians to handle their frustrations in a manner appropriate to their faith. His exegetical idea—"when trials come into your life, use them to grow to maturity"— gets stated in a more pithy fashion in his homiletical idea— "when life deals you a lemon, make a lemonade." To develop this thought, he answers the functional question "What does that mean?" in the three main points of his outline. Like any effective homiletical outline, Cocoris speaks to his audience from James, not about James.

I. You Can Make Lemonade out of a Lemon, If You Are Quick to Hear God's Word.
   A. Be quick to hear God's Word (1:21).
      1. James could be saying that we need to hear others generally (but)
      2. James is saying that we need to hear God's Word in the midst of trial.
   B. Be quick to heed God's Word (1:22–2:26) (which means)
      1. Be swift to help God's people (1:26–27).
      2. Do not shun the poor to honor the rich (2:1–13).
      3. Show your faith in good works (2:14–26).

(The summary of James 1:21–2:26, then, is be swift to hear and heed God's Word by helping God's people.)

II. You Can Make Lemonade out of a Lemon, If You Are Slow to Speak (3:1–18)
   A. Be slow to speak because while the tongue can do great good, it can also do great harm and be inconsistent (3:1–12).
   B. Be slow to speak because wisdom from heaven should be shown first in actions (3:13–18).
III. You Can Make Lemonade out of a Lemon, If You Are Slow to Become Angry (4:1–5:18)
   A. Be slow to wrath because the consequence of a wrong attitude is war (4:1–10).
   B. Be slow to wrath because the consequence of a wrong attitude is judging (4:11–12).
   C. Be slow to wrath because the consequence of a wrong attitude is planning without God (4:13–17).
   D. Be slow to wrath because the consequence of a wrong attitude is a wrong handling of unjust treatment (5:1–12).
   E. Be slow to wrath because the consequence of a wrong attitude is physical illness (5:13–18).

COMMENTARY

233

Conclusion: The way to make lemonade out of a lemon is "be quick to listen, slow to speak, and slow to become angry!"

Covering larger portions of Scripture forces the preacher to sacrifice details to the broader view. After all, if you want to describe the United States, you will not be able to stop to describe individual streets or houses. A survey only allows a minister to state his points, but he cannot take much time to develop them. For example, Cocoris believes that "slow to become angry" sums up the final two chapters of James. Those who need further proof that this concept adequately accounts for James' discussion on making business decisions apart from God (4:13–17) will not be satisfied. Detailed explanation and more thorough exposition has probably been given in the previous sermons of the series.

Handling wider sections of the Bible, however, should not

suck the life out of a sermon and turn it into a spoken outline. Cocoris does not talk to his listeners only about the Book of James, but as in all relevant preaching, he speaks to his audience about their hurts and frustrations from the Book of James. His introduction and conclusion refer to a frustrating and stressful situation with which anyone who has to wait for service can identify. He uses analogies, anecdotes, and personal reflections to join his points to life. While the congregation learns something about the letter from James, they also learn a mature approach to life's irritations, both great and small. That's what preaching of any sort is all about.

COMMENTARY

234

How long does it usually take you to prepare a message?

Let me go into a bit of detail. When I'm going to preach through a book of the Bible, the first thing I do is take a week and go somewhere alone. I take a Greek or Hebrew text, an English translation, a couple of commentaries. I divide the book into its natural literary units, and then I do a logical layout of every one of those units. I then come up with a big idea, an outline, and a tentative title for every paragraph or subsection in the book before I ever preach the first paragraph. When I start preaching through the book, I have all that spade work behind me. I then exegete that paragraph and prepare the sermon. If you count all the time I put into each paragraph, it takes me between ten and twenty hours to do a sermon.

How long did it take you to prepare the message you submitted?

To put this particular message together didn't take as long because I had already preached eighteen messages on the Book of James. I simply had to find supporting material.

How long are your sermons normally?

I rarely preach under thirty-five minutes, and I consistently preach forty to forty-five minutes.

Describe how you do the actual preparation of a sermon.

Prior to preparing a sermon, I have already written out a one-page summary of the historical background. I deliberately keep it to one page. I have also divided the book into its natural literary units. I now do a logical layout in which I'm looking for the literary structure of the particular unit I'll preach on. I trace the development of the thought through the passage and end up with a big idea.

Once I get to the study, I go through the passage by myself first, with only a Greek text in hand. I glean all I can from the passage, then I start reading commentaries. I generally take three of the most technical commentaries, and I underline what I think is pertinent information. By this time, I've got the central idea of the passage and the sermon is taking shape. Also by this time, I have spent a lot of time thinking not only about the passage but about the sermon. Then I come up with an introduction and some idea of where I'm going.

At that point I start writing. I write the introduction. I write in outline form but I write a full text of the sermon. I will start with an explanation. As I come to a place where I think I need an illustration, I either stop and look for one in my illustration file, or I will leave a blank space in the manuscript and come back to it later on. What I'm doing is writing out the explanation of the passage. That alone takes four to five hours.

Where do you get your illustrations?

From everywhere. I read, I rip things out of magazines, I xerox things and have my secretary file them. I have an elaborate filing system: five file drawer cabinets filled with studies I've done, my manuscripts of sermons, all the material I could collect. I started out with a different folder for every book in the Bible and every time I come across something that even remotely relates to that book, I throw it in the folder. I have a 3x5 card system. When I became pastor of this church nine years ago, it was filled with elderly people. I got them to give me back-copies of "Our Daily Bread." Volunteers filed them all by text. I have seven thousand of them. I was on "Day of Discovery" several years ago, and they gave me copies of "Our Daily Bread" I lacked. I have every "Daily Bread" that's ever been published. I will cut out a story and glue it right in the manuscript.

Do you try to tie your introduction and conclusion together?

I don't do it regularly, but I do like to raise a problem in the introduction and answer it at the conclusion.

What was the greatest challenge for you in approaching this sermon?

To make sure that all the details adequately satisfy the big idea, or actually that the big idea satisfies all the details. Both of these statements are true. It would be easy to come up with an idea that is a superficial explanation of the book. The challenge is to be satisfied that your big idea comes from the details of the book.

You preached through the Bible one book to a sermon. How did that go?

My Route 66 series was the most academic thing I've ever done. It was almost lecture, but the people loved it! It took sixty-seven weeks, taking breaks for conferences and the like. It was the longest series I've ever done.

INTERVIEW

237

Chapter 12

Lament for the City of Man
Revelation 17–18

Joel Eidsness

Joel Eidsness has been the pastor of Trinity Bible Church in Phoenix for the past twenty years. He has served as a board member of Young Life in Arizona, Fuller Seminary Extension in Phoenix, and the Greater Phoenix Association of Evangelicals.

When my oldest daughter was seven, we spent an afternoon at the city dump. Our purpose for this excursion was not to dump garbage, but to observe waste. I backed my Oldsmobile up against the mounds of refuse and placed my daughter on its roof. With pencil and paper in hand, I asked her to list every item she could identify. The results were astounding. There was a plastic swimming pool, a barbeque, and several old lawn chairs. There were Barbie dolls, bicycle frames, skatebords, play refrigerators and stoves, radios, televisions . . . everything a young girl dreams of and more.

As we drove back into the city, talking about what we had just observed, we happened to pull alongside a double trailer truck. When I saw its cargo, I could hardly believe my eyes. Piled high atop each trailer were five hunks of scrap metal bundled together. If you had turned anyone of them upside down, you would probably have found "Made In Detroit" stamped on their underbellies. They were hardly in mint condition. And yet, there they were—ten crumpled cars—magnificent object lessons for a father and daughter who, at that very moment, were discussing the value of "things." I can still remember leaning over and reminding my daughter that the beautiful Delta Royale in which we were then riding was ultimately headed for the same scrap heap.

That was a day Kristen and I will never forget. It was a powerful reminder that someday everything we own will be junk. In some city dump the things that have captivated our attention and dominated our lives will smolder beneath a simmering flame, amidst stinking mounds of rotting garbage. But the picture portrays not only the end of our lives and that of our children. It portrays the ultimate collapse of human history as we now know it. History is not destined to grind on forever. It awaits—wittingly or unwittingly—the awesome and terrible judgment of God. Few chapters in the Bible describe this frightful end more pointedly than Revelation 17 and 18 and few people need to hear its message more than we Americans.

In these two chapters the apostle openly acknowledges the power of the material in our lives and warns us to loose ourselves from its grip. Civilization, as we know it, is destined for destruction. Ultimately the city of man must give way to the city of God, the secular city to the Holy City. Babylon must fall, God says; only the New Jerusalem can remain.

These two chapters revolve around the images John sees and the voice he hears. The images are earthly, while the voice is heavenly. We cannot understand the voice apart from the images. If we fail to grasp the essence of these images on earth, we will not adequately heed the voice from heaven.

The first image is that of a seductive mistress (Rev. 17:1–18). Babylon is no ordinary mistress. John refers to her as "the great prostitute" (17:1), "the mother of prostitutes" (17:5). Here is no cheap and tawdry whore who plies her wares on some darkened street; here is a stunning and beautiful woman. Her sleek body models the latest fashions from Herrods in London and Sak's Fifth Avenue in New York. Her neck glitters with gold. Diamonds and precious stones adorn her fingers. She lives not in some sleazy hotel in New Orleans, but in an exquisitely decorated Manhattan penthouse.

This woman is not to be confused with the beast on which

she sits. Though she is energized by him, she is distinct from him. He is an animal; she is a woman. He is a monster; she is a model. He is beastly; she is beautiful. He aims to oppress Christ's church; she to seduce it. Because of her attractive nature, she is to be feared.

Not only is she attractive; she is powerful. John views her as one "who sits on many waters" (17:1). The language is figurative. Its meaning is given in 17:15: "The waters you saw, where the prostitute sits, are peoples, multitudes, nations and languages." Note the plurals. Her power and influence know few limitations. First, she is no respecter of geography; her influence extends to all "nations," united or divided, developing or developed. Second, she is no respecter of humanity; her influence extends to all "peoples, multitudes . . . and languages." This includes commoners as well as kings, ordinary citizens as well as royal nobility (17:2). Finally, she is no respecter of history; her influence extends throughout the whole of time (17:8ff.). This is obvious when we examine the beast on which she sits. That John's beast "was" refers to his activity in the past. That the beast "now is not" refers to his defeat at Calvary. He is a defeated sovereign, an animal on a short leash, if you will. Nevertheless, his ability to resuscitate himself is noted in the words *will yet come.* Evil's resuscitative powers are impressive. How else can you explain the likes of Adolph Hitler, Joseph Stalin, and Idi Amin?

Unlike the beast, however, who persecutes the people of God, this woman seduces them. To embrace her looks as if it will lead to the good life, but her bed has within it the stench of death. John writes that she holds a "golden cup in her hand" (17:4). One would think the cup to be filled with vintage wine, but instead we read that it is filled with "abominable things and the filth of her adulteries." This woman, who is both attractive and powerful, is also destructive. Jim Jones is but one example of this seductive mistress. Jones spoke of human dignity to people who were oppressed. He opposed racial prejudice and proclaimed the value of every person. Followers flocked to the People's Temple expecting to drink from its life-giving chalice. They never expected the cup to be filled with cyanide. So too, this mistress invites us to taste her wares, to drink from her cup, and we do. Trapped in sexual sin, we rationalize, "It's not an affair; it's a relationship." Having tasted the good life we argue, "God wants his people to be rich. After all we're the King's." Wanting to secure our future, we eschew suffering and develop prophetic schemes that will deliver us from pain. But be careful. This mistress is not only attractive and powerful; she is destructive. Love her and you will perish with her. Allow yourself to be seduced by her and you will be reduced to ashes with her (17:16–17).

All that remains is to identify this seductive mistress. A hint as to her identification is given in 17:5: "This title was written on her forehead:

SERMON

244

MYSTERY
BABYLON THE GREAT
THE MOTHER OF PROSTITUTES
AND OF THE ABOMINATIONS OF THE EARTH"

The word *mystery* indicates that she is to be understood figuratively not literally, theologically not politically, symbolically not geographically.

Babylon is not a real city in prophecy waiting to be built. Rather, she is a representative city in history waiting to be destroyed. She stands throughout the Bible for the city of man which is opposed to the city of God. She represents false religion, prideful humanity, and godless society. She stands for the world and all that is in it, "the cravings of sinful man, the lust of his eyes, and the boasting of what he has and does" (1 John 2:16). She represents man and society in opposition against God. In the opening chapters of the Bible, humanity gathered itself together and said, "Come, let us build ourselves a city, with a tower that reaches to the heavens, so that we may make a name for ourselves and not be scattered over the face of the earth" (Gen. 11:4).

But the real question regarding Babylon is where this seductive mistress encounters us. Here I speak personally. Babylon encounters me in my ego. I like the story about the Texan who arrived in heaven. An angel asked if there was anything he could do to make the Texan's stay more enjoyable. The man, who loved music, responded: "Give me ten thousand sopranos." "Anything else?" the angel asked. "Yes, I'd like ten thousand altos, and while you're at it how about getting me ten thousand tenors, too." "Consider it done," said the angel. "Anything else?" "Nope, that'll be it for the present." The angel's curiosity was piqued. So he asked, "Well, how about the bassos?" Answered the Texan, "I'll sing bass." What an apt description of our lives.

In recent years, I've been forced to make some painful mid-life adjustments. Some of my best friends are writing books. They are being invited to speak around the world. And I've had to ask myself, what happened to all of those hopes and dreams I so carefully fashioned during my seminary days? I wanted to be Ray Stedman, Charles Swindoll, Richard Halverson, John Stott, Michael Green, Elisabeth Elliot, and Corrie Ten Boom all wrapped up in one. Often I've had to remind myself of the words of Jesus. Do you want to be first? Then be last. Do you want to win? Then lose. Do you want to be admired by all? Then be the servant of all.

Some of you may be chuckling at the insecurities and ego needs of this preacher. But be careful: pride is a congenital disease; it is a universal malady. As Pascal once wrote, "Vanity is so anchored in the heart of man that those who write against it want to have the glory of having written well and those who read it desire the glory of having read it." And as Saint Francis de Sales added, "Pride will only disappear from the human heart fifteen minutes after we have died." I confess to you, Babylon encounters me in my ego.

Babylon also encounters me in my schedule. Jesus said, "Come to me, all you who are weary and burdened, and I will give you rest" (Matt. 11:28). Believe me, I want to come, I need to come, I long to come—and yet the truth of the matter is, I do not come. My problem is twofold: it is a mixture of busyness and laziness. Television seduces me, a good book captivates me, theological conversation stimulates me, an athletic event excites me, sermon preparation beckons me, while people pursue me. None of these activities is wrong in and of itself, but when one of them lures me away from the presence of God, it is Babylon. If you are at all like me, you will have to confess that it's easier to talk about God than to him, to read books about him than the Book by him. I confess, Babylon encounters me in my schedule.

Furthermore, Babylon encounters me in my possessions. If you miss the material thrust of Revelation 17 and 18, you miss the essence of what God is saying in these chapters. It is the Soviet Union and the Eastern-bloc countries who feel the harsh hand of the beast. But in the West we know only the warm embrace of the woman whose beauty lures us into a dependence upon things. In Revelation 18:12–13 twenty-nine articles are listed. The first article is gold, the last people. That's always the economy of the world: gold first, people last. In the city of God, gold is for paving streets—it's for people to walk on. But in the city of man, people get traded for gold and stepped on for silver. T. S. Eliot was close to the mark when he predicted that one day the epitaph on America's tombstone might well read, "Here lies a decent, godless people. Their only monument to civilization was an asphalt road and a thousand lost golf balls."

John White describes the confusion of my heart—perhaps yours too:

> We would like to believe that our treasure was in heaven and that heaven was our real choice. But . . . earthly treasures continue to attract. We may not want outrageous wealth and would be content with reasonable financial security. . . . But we don't want to miss out on anything either. We are ambivalent. . . . We are like the monkey with his fist trapped inside the coconut shell clutching a fistful of peanuts. The monkey wants freedom and peanuts and he cannot have both.[1]

At times I feel like that monkey. I want God, and. . . .

Where is Babylon encountering you? You may be a Christian

1. John White, *The Golden Cow: Materialism in the Twentieth-Century Church* (Downers Grove, Ill.: Inter-Varsity, 1979), pp. 47–48.

about to marry a non-Christian. You may be involved emotionally, even physically, with someone other than your spouse. You may be launching a business with someone whose morality and ethics you question. You may be involved in a friendship that is slowly but surely dampening your commitment to Christ. I caution you as I caution myself. Babylon is out to seduce you. She is stunningly attractive; she is cunningly powerful; but she is also utterly destructive.

If the first image John sees is that of a seductive mistress, the second image he sees is that of a desolate city.

> After this I saw another angel coming down from heaven. . . . With a mighty voice he shouted: "Fallen! Fallen is Babylon the Great! She has become a home for demons and a haunt for every evil spirit, a haunt for every unclean and detestable bird." (Rev. 18:1–2)

Here the angel announces the collapse of every pagan civilization—past, present, and future. If you want to feel the impact of God's inescapable judgment, read in place of Babylon, "America." "Fallen! Fallen is America, the greatest nation in the modern world!"

Then John is given the reason for the collapse of civilization: "Her sins are piled up to heaven, and God has remembered her crimes" (Rev. 18:5). In Alexander Solzhenitsyn's now famous lecture "Men Have Forgotten God," he chronicles the woes of the Soviet Union:

> More than half a century ago, while I was still a child, I recall hearing a number of old people offer the following explanation for the great disasters that had befallen Russia: "Men have forgotten God. That's why all this has happened." Since then I have spent well-nigh 50 years working on the history of our revolution; in the process I have read hundreds of books, collected hundreds of personal testimonies, and have already contributed eight volumes of my own toward the effort of clearing away the rubble left by that upheaval. But if I were asked today to formulate as concisely as possible the main cause of the ruinous revolution that swallowed up some 60 million of our people, I could not put

it more accurately than to repeat: "Men have forgotten God: that's why all this has happened."[2]

Men have forgotten God. But make no mistake about it: God has not forgotten men. Though, in the West, we boast about our security and make great plans for the future, the Bible warns of the inevitable judgment of God. "In one day her plagues will overtake her: death, mourning and famine. She will be consumed by fire, for mighty is the Lord God who judges her" (Rev. 18:8).

In Revelation 18 there are three separate funeral songs, all choruses of mourning. The first funeral song is sung by the politicians of the earth (vv. 9–10). Their power has come to nought. The city over which their power held sway is burning. The second funeral song is sung by the earth's economists (vv. 11–17a). Wall Street and the World Bank have collapsed. The economists are weeping because there will be no more people to buy their wares. The third funeral song is sung by common laborers—sailors and merchant marines—the trade unionists of the world (vv. 17b–19). They are weeping because they will never again be employed in the world. And while this earthly multitude weeps and mourns, a song of jubilation breaks out in heaven (v. 20). "Rejoice over her, O heaven! Rejoice, saints and apostles and prophets! God has judged her for the way she has treated you." People may forget God, but God never forgets people.

Then a mighty angel takes a large stone, perhaps five to six feet in diameter and a foot thick, weighing thousands of pounds, and hurls it into the sea. Such is the fate of the city of man. Never again will art, music, and the humanities grace her streets. Never again will blue- and white-collar workers ply their trades there. In the city of man silence and darkness will reign. Even the family will be destroyed, for the voice of the bride and bridegroom will not be heard again. The late Lord Louis Mountbatten captured Babylon's demise unknowingly when he wrote of the aftermath of a nuclear explosion:

2. Alexander Solzhenitsyn, "Men Have Forgotten God," *Pastoral Renewal* 8 (April 1984): 116.

And when it is all over what will the world be like? Our fine, great buildings, our homes will exist no more. The thousands of years it took to develop our civilization will have been in vain. Our works of art will be lost. Radio, television, newspapers will disappear. There will be no means of transport. There will be no hospitals. . . . There will be no neighboring towns left, no neighbors, there will be no help, there will be no hope.[3]

I am not advocating that a nuclear holocaust will end the world, only that the aftermath of God's judgment as described by John, will be like the aftermath of a nuclear explosion. This is where the world in which we live is headed. Every civilization, every empire, every culture, every political ideology, every false religion will one day be buried beneath the dust of death. Only the city of God and those who people it are eternally secure. The images John sees are clear. Life lived for self apart from the lordship of Jesus Christ though attractive at first sight, will ultimately self destruct. Babylon is not only a seductive mistress; she is a desolate city.

Against this sure prophecy regarding the collapse of every human institution and culture people ask, "Is there any reason for hope?" John's response is positive, if we pay attention to both the voice he hears and the images he sees. The words thunder forth from heaven: "Come out of her, my people, so that you will not share in her sins, so that you will not receive any of her plagues" (18:4). Come out of her, God says, or you will be destroyed with her. Reject her before she rejects you. Don't allow yourself to be seduced by her or you will be judged with her.

These words obviously require something from us. In brief, God is asking us to identify Babylon. Where are you encountering her? Where is she seducing you? Most of us describe the demise of civilizations spatially or biologically. We speak of the rise and fall of the Roman Empire or the birth and death of the British Empire. But in the Bible the demise of nations and per-

---

3. Quoted in Ron Sider and Richard K. Taylor, *Nuclear Holocaust and Christian Hope: A Book for Christian Peacemakers* (Downers Grove, Ill.: Inter-Varsity, 1982), p. 26.

sons is spiritual. A nation either submits itself to God or rebels against him—and what is true of nations is also true of individuals. Where in your life are you saying yes to God and where are you saying no?

Luther once said, "Whatever your heart clings to and confides in, that is really your God."[4] What or whom do you love more than God? Perhaps it's a child, a spouse, a friend. Perhaps it's a home, an auto, a recreational vehicle. It may be your job, a hobby, even a ministry. Don't ignore it; identify it. Don't hide it; admit it. Don't justify it; acknowledge it. And once it is in the open, deal with it.

Many Westerners breathed a sigh of relief when 1984 came and passed and George Orwell's "big brother" failed to dominate our lives. Neil Postman in *Amusing Ourselves to Death* says that we may have feared the wrong enemy. He contends that Aldous Huxley's *Brave New World* more aptly describes the conditions in the West while Orwell's *1984* better portrays realities behind the Iron Curtain. Postman writes: "Orwell feared that what we hate will ruin us. Huxley feared that what we love will ruin us."[5] As I view twentieth-century America, I agree with Postman: Huxley, not Orwell, perceived the real enemy.

We Americans have not yet seen the beast. We have not yet experienced the iron fist of persecution. We know only this seductive mistress and we have already sensed the warm embrace of her soft flesh. We have not been persecuted; we have been seduced. We have not been brutalized; we have been deceived. If we are going to excise Babylon from our lives, we will do best to examine the aspirations and life-styles we embrace, not those we detest.

However, it's not simply enough to identify Babylon in our lives; we must dethrone her. To dethrone Babylon means to strip her of her sacred character, to topple her from her place of

4. Cited in *The Oxford Dictionary of Quotations,* 3d ed. (New York: Oxford University Press, 1979), p. 320.

5. Neil Postman, *Amusing Ourselves to Death* (New York: Penguin Books, 1985), p. viii.

dominance and power. I share with you how this has been worked out in my own life.

Some years ago I loaned my new Volkswagen Rabbit to a friend visiting from out of town. When he returned it, I noticed that the left front fender had been damaged. When I asked about his accident, I received nothing more than a blank stare. "That's the way you gave it to me," he said. Because I trust this friend implicitly, I knew there had to be another explanation. At the body shop I was surprised to discover it was likely that my Rabbit had been hit while parked. But the most surprising thing about this incident was the new sense of liberation I experienced. With a crumpled left fender the innocence of my Rabbit was gone. She was marred for life. Additional dents and scratches didn't matter any longer. That dent liberated my Rabbit for the kingdom. From then on anybody could borrow her—after all, she was God's automobile, not mine. In reality she had been God's automobile all along; I simply was reluctant to let God use her. How easy it is for the things we own to own us. That is the danger of things. They come to us as a trust from God; we end up trusting in them instead, treating them like a god. That which was intended to be our servant becomes our master.

How can we make sure that things do not enslave us? I respond, "Dethrone them; give them away." "But I have little to give," you say. In a Romanian jail cell Richard Wurmbrand didn't have much either, but material resources would not dominate the whole of his existence. To break its power, he tithed—not cash but food. Every tenth day he and other Christian brothers gave their bread rations away to prisoners more needy than themselves. Why did Wurmbrand do this? I suspect he wanted to demonstrate that Babylon was not his earthly residence. Like John, he wanted to heed the voice from heaven which pleads with us not only to identify Babylon in our lives, but to dethrone her as well. He wanted to strip the material of the power it holds over our lives. Only then could he extricate himself from this world's warm, but deadly embrace.

Why do you cling so tenaciously to Babylon? Why do you pursue things? Why do you spend all your time working and

SERMON

251

worrying about your investments in the city of man? They are headed for destruction, destined for the scrap heap. They will one day smolder beneath a simmering flame amidst stinking mounds of rotting garbage. John says so! " 'With such violence the great city of Babylon will be thrown down, never to be found again' " (Rev. 18:21b).

In *The Great Divorce,* C. S. Lewis tells of a ghost who arrived in Paradise with a lizard attached to his lapel. He was quickly informed by the gatekeeper that lizards were not welcome in the New Eden. He must throw it to the ground and crush it. Only in that brutal act could he show himself worthy of the heavenly city. The ghost agonizes over his decision. This scaly reptile has been his constant companion, his intimate friend. How could he give him up? Could he bear the pain? Would heaven be heaven without this dear friend?[6]

These questions are appropriate for us as well, as we contemplate the seduction and power of Babylon in our lives. If we abandon our dependency upon self, will we find another companion? If we relinquish our grip on things, will we ever again be happy? If we renounce our citizenship in the city of man and pledge allegiance to the city of God, will we experience fulfillment? In Lewis's story the man in the end finally tears the lizard from his lapel and throws it to the ground. Despite its grievous cries for help, he crushes it beneath his feet. At that very moment the reptile is metamorphosed. Rising from the ground, this beastly creature is transformed into a powerful horse, and it is on this animal that the ghost rides into the heavenly city. Lewis's story echoes the invitation of Jesus: " 'If anyone would come after me, he must deny himself and take up his cross and follow me. For whoever wants to save his life will lose it, but whoever loses his life for me and for the gospel will save it' " (Mark 8:34b–35).

If you doubt the truth of these words, I invite you to take a short but purposeful trip. Drive out to your city dump. Back your Nissan Sentra, your Buick Regal, or your BMW up against the mounds of rotting garbage. See what others have discarded. Are

6. C. S. Lewis, *The Great Divorce* (New York: Macmillan, 1958), pp. 99–107.

not many of the smoldering items things you've worked hard to acquire? Watch them burn. Let the awesome stench of that dump pass through your nostrils. Are not the signs of Babylon's ultimate collapse most obvious here? God cautions us—indeed pleads with us:

> Do not love the world or anything in the world. If anyone loves the world, the love of the Father is not in him. For everything in the world—the cravings of sinful man, the lust of his eyes and the boasting of what he has and does—comes not from the Father but from the world. The world and its desires pass away, but the man who does the will of God lives forever. (1 John 2:15–17)

Stop embracing Babylon. Reject her before she rejects you. Renounce your allegiance to the city of man and pledge allegiance to the city of God. Babylon will self destruct. Only the city of God will endure. "He is no fool who gives up what he cannot keep to gain what he cannot lose."

SERMON

253

Commentary

No book of the Bible fascinates—or bewilders—readers more than the Book of Revelation. George Bernard Shaw dismissed it as "the curious record of the visions of a drug addict." Many of the more devout, living in the shadow of the second coming, perceive in it a detailed summary of religious, political, and military actions leading up to the return of Jesus Christ. The curious speculate about its images; theologians argue over its interpretation; adventists, Seventh Day and otherwise, found denominations on it; and in spite of the assurance of blessing to those who ponder it, preachers often approach it like an illiterate with a crossword puzzle. Revelation is not a simple book to preach.

In his sermon, Joel Eidsness expounds Revelation 17–18, one of the more difficult sections of this perplexing book. The initial reading of these chapters raises questions about how to interpret apocalyptic literature and the meaning of John's vision of a prostitute riding on a ferocious beast. Eidsness sees in this episode the ultimate destruction of the present world order, a system which lures us away from God by appealing to the cravings of our bodies, our desire for more and more of what we have enough of already, and our lust for recognition and power.

Homiletically, his sermon applies a principle to men and women who want to take God seriously. "We should identify the power of Babylon over our lives and dethrone her." Eidsness's development is clear and easy to understand. He first identifies Babylon in the Bible and in our experience and then offers two compelling reasons for overthrowing its seductions.

I. Babylon Stands for the Civilization in Which We Live.
    A. Babylon appeals to us like a seductive mistress.
        1. The mistress is attractive.
        2. The mistress is powerful.
        3. The mistress is destructive.
    B. Babylon, representing people and society opposed to God, encounters us in different areas of our lives.
        1. Babylon encounters us in our ego.
        2. Babylon encounters us in our schedule.
        3. Babylon encounters us in our possessions.
    C. Babylon is a desolate city under judgment because of her sins.
        1. The death of Babylon will be mourned by three funeral songs sung by politicians, economists, and common laborers.
        2. The destruction of the city will be complete.

(How then should we respond to the influence of Babylon in our lives?)

II. We Must Identify Babylon's Influence in Our Lives and Dethrone Her.
    A. Babylon and what she represents is destined for destruction.
    B. Only the city of God will endure.

The effectiveness of this sermon evolves not only from its thought but also through its development. Although in general terms the passage tells us what John saw and then what John heard, Eidsness chooses not to follow that structure in his sermon. Instead he handles his material in a logical or psychological order. An expository preacher is free to work the biblical material in any manner that will tellingly communicate the message of a text to the listener. After all, the test of whether a sermon is expository does not necessarily depend on whether it goes through a passage verse by verse, but whether it opens up the text to reflect the meaning and emphasis of a biblical author.

Eidsness keeps a strong sense of tension throughout the sermon. When tension is lost, a sermon is over (even if the preacher takes thirty minutes more to get to the conclusion). Throughout a well-designed sermon new questions are raised that require answers. For example, Eidsness's major transition bridging the two main movements of his message is such a question: Why should we dethrone the influence of Babylon in our lives? Not only is this the preacher's question, but at this point in the sermon it should be the congregation's question as well. In fact, the entire sermon from the introduction through to the conclusion forces a perceptive listener to deal with the insidious and destructive influence of civilization on our lives.

This sermon strikes life in many ways—by the way it is developed, by suggesting the seductions Babylon makes to us, and by the constant use of strong illustrations. Eidsness makes himself transparent through references to his own particular vulnerability to the appeal of the world system, and, by that self-revelation, demonstrates that not even religious leaders are exempt from the enticement to swear allegiance as citizens of Babylon.

While the sermon deals with ancient literature and also anticipates the future, Eidsness's supporting material plants it firmly in the current life of his people. Quotations from Alexander Solzhenitsyn, Lord Louis Mountbatten, George Orwell, Aldous Huxley, and C. S. Lewis, along with allusions to places like Sak's Fifth Avenue in New York, Herrods in London, "some sleazy hotel in New Orleans," a "Manhattan penthouse" and references to people like Jim Jones, Adolph Hitler, Joseph Stalin, and Idi Amin tell us that this sermon, and the interpretation that prompted it, does not deal with distant times or future vistas.

The wording of the sermon also adds to its impact. Like the apocalyptic literature itself, Eidsness's way of stating things flashes emotional images on the wall of the mind. Starting with his opening account of a visit to a city dump, his style stimulates the senses of sight, smell, touch, and hearing. "Smolder beneath a simmering flame," "stinking mounds of rotting garbage," "history is not destined to grind on forever"—these phrases selected from a single page reach out to the imagination through the senses. Such wording produces miniature illustrations which stamp a sermon on the feelings as well as the intellect.

COMMENTARY

How long does it usually take you to prepare a message?

Between fifteen and twenty hours on a Sunday morning message.

How long did it take you to prepare the message you submitted?

When it comes to the Book of Revelation, covering chapters 17 and 18 with their phenomenal interpretive complexities, I probably spent considerably more time. But I don't remember now. I invest another ten to twelve hours on my Sunday evening message.

How long are your sermons normally?

Thirty-five minutes.

How do you go about the preaching task?

I begin with a preaching calendar. Six months ahead I try to work through the segment of the text I am going to cover. Generally, I don't preach through a book. I break a series up. I did Revelation 1–11 then waited over a year to do Revelation 12–22. When I come to the week of the sermon, I start with the text. I spend time reading. I'm a heavy commentary man; I particularly like commentaries that are fairly academic and scholarly. I utilize Bible dictionaries. I also index journals on 3x5 cards. As I read, I attempt to get a grasp of what is happening in the biblical text. Then I ask myself, "What is the connecting link with my people?" "Where does this text arrest my congregation in the contemporary setting where they live?" I look for key words. Then I try to develop an outline, one that will not only grasp the text, but will help me communicate what it says to my people. I didn't do an outstanding job on the outline for this message; I would have liked to have transferred this into a more contemporary outline.

Where do you get your illustrations?

I try to draw illustrations from life, especially my experiences with people. I enjoy reading and try to read broadly: novels, Michael O'Conner, Solzhenitsyn, Postman, journals, magazines, reviews. I keep four to five books going at a time. Films and movies make great illustrative resources. Friends also give me illustrations.

How do you get effective introductions to your sermons?

I ask, "How can I grab my people's attention?" Right off the bat I have to give them something that isn't "ho-hum." Second, somewhere in the introduction I have to arouse in them the reality to which this text speaks. The illustration of my daughter not only tried to grab attention, but I think aroused the kinds of needs this passage addresses. All the things we work so hard to achieve are one day going to end up in the garbage dump.

Your conclusion referred back to your introduction. Do you do this regularly?

I do try to tie things together so there is some thematic flow between how I start and how I close, but I don't always "start with a dump and end with a dump." I do try, in the conclusion, as well as in the introduction, to keep the sermon flowing as a single unit.

What difficulties emerged in handling the biblical text of this sermon?

The complexity. "Babylon" is difficult to define. I had to grapple with diverse interpretations and settle on how I saw Babylon in that passage. Its length also made it difficult—over forty verses in those two chapters. Then, I wrestled with its relevance. So much in the Book of Revelation is futuristic. So I had to ask myself, "What relevance does this book have to today?"

Would you consider this a "principle-applied" message?

If Revelation is both idealistic and futuristic as I think it is, then the author intended for us to see Babylon not only as something at the end of time, but to look for it throughout all history. Isn't that what we do with Babylon as we see it in the Old Testament? Not one literal city, but representative of every city opposed to God. So this is an "idea explained" because I state my purpose in the introduction. Most of my dispensational friends might say it is a "principle-applied" sermon, because they see the Book of Revelation only as futuristic. I see the Book of Revelation neither as a prophetic horoscope nor an unsolvable puzzle, but as a book of symbols and pictures very relevant for the culture we live in. It is both symbolic and literal.

You identify Babylon with our modern civilization. How did you arrive at that conclusion?

The biblical data helped me. Babylon in the Bible refers not only to literal cities, but also to representative cities. Genesis 11, the tower of Babel, stands for an entity opposed to God. Isaiah 13 speaks of the destruction of Babylon before the time of Christ. But the apocalyptic language also refers to the end of the world. The double images pointed both to the near future when literal Babylon would be destroyed and to any city throughout history. Babylon is used as a symbol throughout the Bible. Therefore, in the Book of Revelation I see two major cities—Babylon, the city of man, that puts its fist in God's face, and the new Jerusalem, the city of God, coming out of heaven. In Revelation, those two cities are pitted against one another. That is what led me to identify Babylon with modern civilization. The city of man shakes its fist in God's face. Every civilization becomes that Babylon. This message speaks with relevance to every culture.

You didn't spend much time explaining all that in your sermon. Why not?

Most of my people are not interested in heavy interpretive data. To spend a long time explaining how I identify Babylon doesn't satisfy them very much.

How do you develop your good wording?

I work hard at it. I find that, first, you can't read good literature and not have it affect you. I've longed for that kind of skill. I have a high view of writing.

As you look back at your classes in homiletics, what were the most helpful lessons you learned?

First, the importance of a preaching calendar. Second, the importance of an illustration file. Third, the importance of having a central idea.

Affairs, extramarital, 35, 36–37, 39
Angry wife, 228

Big Joe, 164–65
Boy at supper table, 225

Commuter communication, 153

Dionysius, 207
Dollhouse and father, 71

Evangelistic association, 227

Furniture, undelivered, 223–24, 228–30

Ghost in Paradise, 252
Great Blondin, 209

Hitchhiking hippie, 158

Hot air balloon, 98–99

Immigrant in the army, 203–4

Jim Croche song, 93
Jones, Jim, 243

Kangaroo in Gucci jacket, 159

Lamb clothed in skin, 210
Living in a mansion, 205–6
Little Bo Peep, 159, 163
Lost check, 161
Lost dog, 162, 163
Lost son, 164

Marital fidelity, 33

Nuclear holocaust, 249

Parenting, 101

Partying, 156–57
Piggyback ride, 97, 99
Preacher in penitentiary, 15–16

Ruth and Naomi, 21

Sacrifice of elevator operator, 208
Simple plan of salvation, 211–12
Sisyphus, 97–98
Socrates, 91
Summoned by Bells, 95–96

Teenager and dental appointment, 204
Texan in heaven, 245

Visit to city dump, 241–42
Volkswagen Rabbit, 251

Wurmbrandy's tithing, 251

Index

Alliteration, 42
Application, 29, 63, 67, 130–31, 146, 196
Audience, 10, 25, 42–43, 48, 63, 106

Bible, influence on sermon preparation, 9–10
Biblical preaching, 43
Big idea, 24, 25, 41, 62, 112, 177, 237

Central idea of the sermon. See Big idea.
Commentaries, use of, 29, 45, 46, 109–10, 128
Conclusion of the sermon, 25, 48, 125, 130–31, 260

Deductive preaching, 62, 87, 125

Evangelistic preaching, 213–14, 217, 218–19
Expository preaching, 43, 143, 257

Forms of sermons, 11, 23, 41, 107, 143–44, 193–94: dramatic monologue, 81–83, 144, 146, 149–50; idea-explained, 261; principle-applied, 107, 112; proposition-proved, 41, 194; story-told, 62; subject-completed, 23

Illustrations, 24, 25, 29, 86–87, 129, 148, 170–71, 175–76, 199, 214–15
Inductive preaching, 62–63, 87, 125
Introduction of the sermon, 24, 47, 66–67, 86, 111, 129–30, 149, 176, 260

Key word, 42, 48

Narrative sermons, 61–63, 81–83
Notes, use of, 30

Outlining, 30, 45–46, 61–62, 174

Parables, preaching on, 167–68, 174, 176
Poetry, biblical, 105
Preaching calendar, 65, 147–48, 259
Preparation, methods of, 28–29, 45, 48, 65–66, 127–28, 132, 145, 147–48, 173–74, 235, 236

Relevance, 25, 42, 123, 130

Textual issues, 194–95, 198
Transitions, 25, 30

Variety in preaching, 10–11, 67

Wording of the sermon, 25, 62–63, 175, 258